The Letters of Denise Levertov and William Carlos Williams

New Directions publishes all of the poetry
of Denise Levertov and William Carlos Williams.
Please write for a free complete catalog.

*The Letters of Denise Levertov
and William Carlos Williams*

Edited by Christopher MacGowan

A NEW DIRECTIONS BOOK

Acknowledgments appear on p. 165.

Book design by Erik Rieselbach
Manufactured in the United States of America
New Directions Books are printed on acid-free paper
First published clothbound in 1998
Published simultaneously in Canada by Penguin Books Canada Limited

Library of Congress Cataloging in Publication Data

Levertov, Denise, 1923–1997
The Letters of Denise Levertov and William Carlos Williams /
  edited by Christopher MacGowan.
    p.   cm.
Includes index.
ISBN 0-8112-1392-7 (alk. paper)
    1.   Levertov, Denise, 1923–1997–Correspondence.
    2.   Women poets, American–20th century–Correspondence.
    3.   Williams, William Carlos, 1883–1963–Correspondence.
    I.   Williams, William Carlos, 1883–1963.
    II. MacGowan, Christopher J. (Christopher John).
    III. Title.
PS3562.E8876Z49   1998
811'.54—dc21   98-34194
[b]   CIP

New Directions Books are published for James Laughlin
by New Directions Publishing Corporation
80 Eighth Avenue, New York 10011

CONTENTS

EDITOR'S INTRODUCTION

The close friendship that grew up between William Carlos Williams and Denise Levertov during a decade of visits and correspondence came at a turning point in both their lives. One, nearing the end of a publishing career that stretched back to 1909, was experiencing in the 1950s, for the first time, widespread notice of his achievement. The other, starting out in a new country and reshaping her poetics in fundamental ways, had just one early book behind her—although within a few years she would receive some of the success and recognition that had taken Williams most of a lifetime to gain.

Levertov told in a number of places her story of discovering Williams's work. As she recalled in an essay on Robert Duncan, she purchased Williams's 1949 *Selected Poems* from "the American bookstore on the Rue Soufflot, near the Sorbonne." Levertov initially had difficulty knowing how to read the poems, and only recognized fully their importance to her own work once she moved to the United States. In the early 1950s, she recalled, "I was reading a great deal and taking in at each breath the air of American life. William Carlos Williams became the most powerful influence on my poetry" (*PW*, p. 67). In her last published interview (with Nicholas O'Connell, quoted in *Poets & Writers* [May/June 1998]), conducted two months before her death, she remembered:

> He was very fond of me.... Williams was a sort of gate-
> way into my own development as a poet. He opened up a
> new way of handling language. His essays and ideas
> were important and influential for me too. And when I
> got to know him, he became a wonderful friend.

Williams never published a review or an essay about Levertov's poetry, as he did for a number of the younger poets who also to vary-ing degrees looked to his work as a guide for their own (poets in-cluding Allen Ginsberg, Irving Layton, Robert Lowell, and Louis Zukofsky). But his affection and admiration of her poetry are evi-denced in letters to a number of his correspondents, as well as in the letters to Levertov herself. In a 1956 essay on Charles Olson, Wil-liams described Levertov (although without naming her) as "a woman whose critical judgment I much admire for her own out-standing critical and poetic achievements. One of the best younger writers of my acquaintance." This admiration increased through the decade. "I haven't had in years," Williams wrote to the Guggenheim Foundation in 1960 in support of Levertov's work, "the conviction of energy and chained power that this woman gives me."

In their correspondence—which spanned from 1951 until 1962, when it became impossible for Williams to physically write or type a letter—Levertov grows from admirer, to pupil, to equal. Her obituary essay in *The Nation* led James Laughlin to float the idea in a letter to her that she write the first biography of Williams. Al-though this was not a suggestion that she took up, Levertov's con-tinuing response to Williams's work and legacy extended from the tribute she offered at a poetry reading at the University of Rhode Island on the day of his death to a number of talks and essays over more than thirty years. In her poetry, Levertov's often anthologized "September, 1961" and "For Floss" (sent to Florence Williams with a 1964 letter), as well as "Williams: An Essay" (1982), are important parts of this ongoing response. Levertov's sense of the place of Wil-liams's letters in this legacy can be gauged from her choosing to read from them at the 1966 tribute to Williams that she and Robert Lowell presented at the 92nd St. Y. in New York, and from her subsequently publishing a larger selection of them in *Stony Brook* in 1968. (At the 1966 tribute she also read eight of Williams's poems — all from his later work — "The Pink Locust," "Hunters in the Snow," "The Woodthrush," "Paul," "The Dance," "The Turtle," "Heel & Toe to the End," and "Poem [the rose fades].")

Levertov continued to write to his widow, Florence Williams (who died in 1976), correspondence which is included in this edition. These later letters record not only the affection that Levertov felt for Florence Williams on her own account, but also the way that thinking about Williams remained an important part of a life marked by increasing fame and success, political activism, and domestic tensions.

In his correspondence with Levertov, Williams is direct about what he admires in her poetry, and also about what he finds less satisfying — although critical commentary is by no means all one way. In addition to the poems that Williams encountered in journals, and in the books that Levertov inscribed to him as they were published, she sent him or brought with her on her visits to Rutherford over forty poems, poems now filed with the correspondence at the Beinecke Library. A number of these elicit specific comment from Williams in his letters. But in lieu of the more extended comments on Levertov's work that a review or essay by Williams would have provided, this volume includes the three statements that Williams sent to the Guggenheim Foundation in 1955, 1958, and 1960, statements increasingly informed, detailed, and supportive, as he makes his case for the value of Levertov's work.

The correspondence begins with what amounts to a fan letter from Levertov in Italy, and it catches Williams in a despondent mood. Following her marriage to Mitchell Goodman in 1947, and some time in Paris and Florence, Levertov came to New York in 1948. The two returned to Europe in December 1950 to again live in France and Italy, before sailing back to New York on February 15,

1952. An entry in Levertov's diary from July 9, 1950, now at Stanford, records the couple's joint interest in Williams's work:

> William Carlos Williams an important discovery for us
> both. Mitch constantly reading 'In the American Grain'.
> I, so far, have read only some of the poems. Probably
> more important to Mitch than to me. But the style of the
> poems, their hard honesty, each a core not a vague aura—
> that is a revelation to me. It is the fact of his being so
> specifically American that gives his work even more
> value, at present, to Mitch of course. The history I can
> barely understand in my ignorance & rootlessness.

Robert Creeley, who had known Goodman at Harvard, where Goodman had been Editorial Chairman of *The Harvard Crimson*, supplied Williams's address for the first letter. Creeley, himself in France with his family in 1951, wrote to Williams: "Good that Denise Goodman wrote; they were here when we first came, past friends, etc., and they liked your work very, very much. The husband is writing a novel, etc. Very sure man, very conscious. Anyhow, the ones that count" (January 24, 1952, Beinecke). Goodman— who remained a lifelong enthusiast of Williams's work—visited the poet the following year in Rutherford, along with Cid Corman. A letter from Corman to Williams tells of one consequence:

> Dennie Levertov... was tremendously moved and heartened by our account of your response to her work, and
> Floss's. An increase in confidence is likely to go a long
> way with her. I know you will like her very much as a
> person too, when you meet her. She has a lovely voice, as
> all the Welsh seem to have, though she is extremely shy
> in showing it. Your suggestion that I read her work publicly and perhaps the work of others is a good one" (October 9, 1953, Beinecke).

Levertov herself enthusiastically described her first visit to Williams in a letter to her parents (December 7, 1953):

About the visit to Williams. Well, he & his wife (both young-looking 70 – she white haired tho' possibly a few years younger, he grey but a passable 55 when animated) were absolutely marvellous to us. He made me read and was *so* enthusiastic – said actually that of any poet he knew, now writing, I had the best sense of music and "the subtle measure needed for our time" etc. etc.... About one poem ("The Rights"...) – his wife said to him – "I only wish you'd written it yourself!" !! We are to go again in 10 days or so, with Nik, at their request.

Williams and Levertov were soon able to help one another. Levertov told her parents of the reading problems that Williams's strokes had caused him, and she put him in touch with a teacher whose counselling helped give him the confidence and ability to return to public readings. Williams's encouragement of her work, in turn, helped Levertov have faith in the new direction that her writing was taking. Particularly important was the letter from Williams of August 23, 1954, as she told him in her reply, and as a diary entry from around October 1955, a year later, confirms. Among a number of "guides for the immediate future in pursuing my resolves for work" she lists Williams's "letter... in which he urged me to write, to begin, not to sit waiting – at least I took it to mean that."

In addition to comments on each other's poetry, topics of their correspondence went on to include the work of other contemporary poets, the appearance of new magazines, the painting of Leland Bell, the New York premiere of *Waiting for Godot,* Levertov's first meeting with Robert Duncan, the range of Levertov's responses to living in Mexico (including witnessing a performance by the innovative Poesía en Voz Alta group), and her attending Williams's play *Many Loves* at the Living Theater in New York. Ongoing narratives within the letters include Mitchell Goodman's attempts to find a publisher for his war novel; the publication of Levertov's first American poetry volumes; her Guggenheim applications; and the gradual emergence of her confidence to engage Williams in critical dialogue.

As the correspondence develops, Levertov's field of acquaintance grows as her career takes off, while Williams becomes increasingly house-bound. Reluctant to see visitors because of the communication problems caused by recurring strokes, he also could only type letters with extreme difficulty.

Of course, the letters represent only part of the direct exchanges between these two writers, and the written record is itself incomplete. Although this volume includes all known letters, there are clearly letters missing. "Another wonderful letter from William Carlos Williams" Levertov wrote to her parents on Good Friday, 1954, but the letter was not part of the cache that Levertov put in a bank vault in the 1960s, photocopied for Florence Williams in 1968, or was able to include in the material that went into Special Collections at Stanford University in the late 1980s. And internal evidence in the letters suggests various lacunae.

Levertov's almost legendary discomfort with extended conversations on the telephone no doubt contributed to the richness of the written record that we do have. But she visited Williams in Rutherford on many occasions, and the letters make reference to the pleasure both gained from these face-to-face discussions. In an interview recorded around 1976, and included in Linda Wagner's *Denise Levertov: In Her Own Province,* Levertov recalled: "Like a fool I didn't keep notes of those conversations because they always seemed so impressive, so exhilarating, how could I possibly forget them? And it was a great mistake, because I have a very bad memory, and all I was left with was a general impression of the exhilaration.... They were wonderful meetings." Nevertheless, some flavor of these encounters can be traced. A diary entry from late 1960, or 1961, records Williams rising passionately to insist, to Levertov and another visiting poet, "Damn it, the poem is no place for diffidence! (And he added: 'Ya gotta go WHAM!' hitting one hand with the fist of the other)." Williams's concession to Levertov's point about her poem "The Jacob's Ladder," recorded in a letter of November 1960, gives another indication of the discussions at 9 Ridge Road. While from another visit, she records that Williams shared with her a note left with the post by the mailman—an affectionate parody of "The Red Wheelbarrow" and perhaps a comment too on the volume of the poet's mail:

> So much depends, too
> Upon the cold mailhandler,
>
> Crazed with
> Frost blister
>
> Dumping out the
> Drab mail sack

For Williams, Levertov was an example of what he came to see in the last years of his life as a vindication of his career-long claims for a distinctive American poetry, and an endorsement of the value of the culture itself: no longer one that produced such exiles as James, Pound, Eliot—the whole stream of expatriates who left for Europe in the 1920s, and against whom to some extent Williams had defined his claims for "the local" and "the American idiom" in his own critical statements. As has often been told, the 1950s saw Williams become central to the work of Black Mountain College, the Beat poets, and to a number of other writers. But Levertov had come from the English tradition. While Auden had not conformed to Williams's hopes for poetic conversion when in the 1940s he had reversed the expatriate's transatlantic journey, in Levertov Williams found a poet eager to listen and respond. Williams's letters to the Guggenheim Foundation reveal how much Levertov's coming out of the English tradition was central to his reading of the younger poet and her development, even to the extent of his coloring biographical details and motives to support this reading.

But when, in his letters, Williams placed Levertov in such a role overtly, it was not one that she accepted uncritically—or, at times, at all. As one example of her independence, in her essay "Rilke as Mentor" Levertov comments on her continuing high regard for the German-Austrian poet against the indifference and even hostility of the American poets who were important to her. The general issue becomes central with Williams when he attempts to win her over to his claims for "the American idiom," producing from Levertov an impassioned assertion of her multicultural roots and of her continuing determination to incorporate them into her voice and subject matter. As Levertov's comments on Williams's poetics elsewhere make clear, while she found his concept of "the variable foot" a valuable one, she did not accept the necessity of tying it to American speech, particularly in her own case. Williams himself never completely concedes the point, as his subsequent letters and the Guggenheim recommendations attest.

The correspondence lasted long enough for both poets to be able to look back during Williams's lifetime and offer each other more than one summary of the value of the friendship and its written exchanges. But fortunately, the annotations to this edition can also include a number of later responses and notations to the correspondence made by Levertov over time. One source of responses comes from the 92nd St. Y tribute in 1966, both from the selection of letters that Levertov made, and the comments that she offered while reading them—and also the larger selection made for *Stony Brook*. Levertov also added annotations to the photocopies of Williams's letters that she forwarded to Florence Williams in 1968, copies that are now in the Rutherford Public Library. A few further short notes accompanied the deposit of the letters in the late 1980s, along with her other papers, at Stanford University. And finally, the preparation of this edition provided another opportunity for comment, an opportunity that she was kind enough to take up with enthusiasm in what turned out to be the final weeks before her death on December 20, 1997. The responses were found among Levertov's papers by Paul Lacey, her literary executor.

≈≈≈

As noted above, this edition collects all of the known correspondence between Levertov and Williams, as well as that between Levertov and Florence Williams, although I have omitted two or three items such as Christmas cards that contain merely perfunctory greetings and no message. The correspondence comes from four sources: Levertov's letters to William Carlos and/or Florence Williams are mostly at the Beinecke Library, Yale University, although number 96 is from the Rutherford N.J. Public Library collection, and numbers 44, 79–80, 84, 88, 93–94, 97, and 103 are held by the Manuscripts Department, Lilly Library, Indiana University. All of the letters from Williams to Levertov are from her papers at Stanford University. I am grateful to all of these libraries, the Library of Congress, and the Olin Library, Washington University, St. Louis, for permission to publish materials held in their collections, and also to the John Simon Guggenheim Memorial Foundation for permission to publish Williams's letters in support of Levertov. Part or all of letters 2–4, 8, 10, 17–18, 21, 23–24, 35–36, 43 and 58, all by Williams, appeared in *Stony Brook* 1–2 (Fall 1968), and Levertov had earlier read extracts from letters 2–4, 8, 10, 23–24, and 36 at the 92nd St Y tribute in 1966.

All of Williams's letters were written from his Rutherford home, 9 Ridge Road, often on printed stationary, and unless Williams typed out his address in the letter I have not reproduced it. I have applied the same principle to the letters from Florence Williams, who sent two short notes from vacation addresses. On the other hand, Levertov's life at this time took her to many places, and she almost always recorded the address at the beginning of a letter. Where she has not, or in the case of one incomplete letter where the first page is not available, I have noted her place of residence at the time.

As noted above, part of the interest of this correspondence lies in the poems that Levertov forwarded to Williams. Unfortunately, the forty-six poems, in typescript and manuscript, filed along with the letters in the Beinecke collection are grouped separately from the letters themselves, apparently through a combination of the actions of Williams himself and of a cataloger at the Beinecke. A handwritten list accompanying the material contains a series of speculations on which poems went with which letters, but the entries do not stand up to such evidence as the dates of the poems, internal references in the letters themselves, or inspection of the paper, pen, or typewriter used on the various individual sheets or groups of poems. In addition, many of the letters are misdated in this list (Levertov often omitted the year when dating a letter), and this has contributed to the list's inaccuracy. A full list of the poems filed with the correspondence at the Beinecke Library appears in Appendix C to this edition, and where I have been able to connect a poem or group of poems to a particular letter this information appears as part of that letter's annotations, although sometimes this is merely a suggestion. Of course, some poems would be associated with visits to Williams rather than letters. The list also includes the few Williams poems that are filed with Levertov's papers at Stanford.

Almost all of Levertov's letters to Williams are handwritten, and pose no major editorial problems. I have corrected slips of the pen — spelling errors, a small number of proper names — but have kept her combination of British and American spelling, her hyphenation, and her occasional use of a French word with accents in place of the same English word. Levertov sometimes had afterthoughts before mailing a letter, or the wish to clarify a sentence or two, and the additional comments would not appear in a postscript but be squeezed into a margin at the side of the page, or — marked with an asterisk — added to the bottom. I have not tried to reproduce the spacing of the letter in these instances, but have inserted the additional comments in square brackets into the body of the letter alongside the text it refers to, along with an explanatory note.

Williams's letters are another matter. Throughout the 1950s, as noted earlier, Williams struggled with physical handicaps that made the coordination necessary for typing a constant struggle for him. At times, in addition to misspelling, his punctuation is erratic, the syntax takes off in a direction that becomes difficult to follow, or Williams repeats words or phrases as if collecting his thoughts again before continuing with his point. Only in the very few cases where the result changes meaning in a way that Williams clearly did not intend have I interfered editorially with syntax, repetitions or punctuation. Although I have corrected spelling, I have let stand Williams's erratic capitalization of proper names. It seemed to me that when there is no loss of intended meaning, leaving such characteristics retains something of the flavor of the letters themselves and the struggle, and determination, of the man behind them. In rare cases, which are noted in square brackets, I have speculated on the word Williams may have intended.

The annotations, in addition to identifying (where possible) the personal and literary figures and events alluded to in the letters, also include, as noted above, a number of the annotations and comments that Levertov herself made concerning the letters at various times. I have also included occasionally what I hope is a pertinent comment from a figure mentioned in the letters, either from correspondence in connection with the preparation of this edition, or from published or unpublished comments made elsewhere. I would like to thank Robert Creeley and Elizabeth McFarland Hoffman for permission to quote from their letters to me, Cid Corman and Robert Creeley for permission to quote from their correspondence with Williams, and Paul Lacey for his invaluable assistance. In addition, I am very grateful to the following individuals who took the trouble to answer queries connected with the correspondence: Robert Bertholf, William Davis, John Dollar, Barbara Epler, Peggy Fox, Ralph S. Graber, Nikolai Goodman, Charles Hanna, John Huss, Leila Javitch, Monika Kaup, Joseph R. Keller, Kenneth Price, Liana Sakelliou (whose bibliography of Levertov's work proved invaluable), Tim Schulte, Mary Ellen Solt, Albert Waller, Julia Walker, Emily Wallace, Eliot Weinberger, Mimi Williams, and Jochen Wierich. As the annotations illustrate, my biggest debt is to Denise Levertov herself.

I am very grateful to the following librarians and their staffs for assistance: Anne Posega, Olin Library, Washington University in St. Louis; Laura Moriarty, San Francisco State University, American Poetry Archives; Joseph Cahoon, Harry Ransom Humanities

Research Center, University of Texas at Austin; Maureen Heher and Patricia Willis, Beinecke Rare Book and Manuscript Library, Yale University; Miriam Sawyer, the Rutherford Public Library; Saundra Taylor, the Lilly Library, Indiana University; Steve Siegel, Unterberg Poetry Center, 92nd St. Y; Sara Timby, Special Collections, Stanford University Library; Department of Special Collections and Archives, Kent State University; Inter-Library Loans, Swem Library, College of William and Mary; Special Collections, Alderman Library, University of Virginia, and G. Thomas Tanselle, Vice President of the John Simon Guggenheim Memorial Foundation. The College of William and Mary provided helpful support for my travel to the collections at Stanford and Yale.

— *Christopher MacGowan*

Key figures, library collections, letter types, and works frequently cited in the notes have been identified by the following abbreviations:

DL   Denise Levertov
FW   Florence Williams
MG   Mitchell Goodman
WCW   William Carlos Williams

B   Beinecke Library, Yale University
RPL   Rutherford Public Library
S   Stanford University Libraries

ACardS   autograph card signed
ALS   autographed letter signed
TLS   typed letter signed
TPC   typed postcard

A   *The Autobiography of William Carlos Williams.* New York: Random House, 1951; reprint, New York: New Directions, 1967
ARI   *A Recognizable Image: William Carlos Williams on Art and Artists.* Edited by Bram Dijkstra. New York: New Directions, 1978
CEP   Denise Levertov, *Collected Earlier Poems 1940–1960.* New York: New Directions, 1979
CP1   William Carlos Williams, *Collected Poems: Volume I, 1909–1939.* Edited by A. Walton Litz and Christopher MacGowan. New York: New Directions, 1986
CP2   William Carlos Williams, *Collected Poems: Volume II, 1939–1962.* Edited by Christopher MacGowan. New York: New Directions, 1988
HN   Denise Levertov, *Here and Now.* San Francisco: City Lights Books, 1957
JL   Denise Levertov, *The Jacob's Ladder.* New York: New Directions, 1961

THE LETTERS
OF DENISE LEVERTOV
AND WILLIAM CARLOS WILLIAMS

THE LETTERS
OF DENISE LEVERTOV
AND WILLIAM CARLOS WILLIAMS

1. TLS-1

[Oct./Nov. 1951]
8 via Cavour
SORI
NR. GENOA
Italy.

Dear William Carlos Williams,

I stopped myself from writing to you for a long time because of a self-conscious idea that it might seem my motive was to draw attention to myself, collect your autograph, or something like that. But I've decided this is silly. If a man is a force in one's life, as you are in mine & my husband's, if his work has given not only great pleasure & excitement but is felt to enter the fabric of one's thinking & feeling & one's way of trying to work, he certainly ought to know it. So, thank you.

yours sincerely,
Denise Levertov Goodman.

I got the address from
Bob Creeley.

"This letter ... was the 1st direct contact I had with W.C.W." Note by DL filed with this letter at S.

DL and MG (1924–1997) had lived in Paris and Florence after their December 2, 1947, marriage, before moving to New York in 1948. In 1950 they went back to Europe, living in Aix-en-Provence, France, and Italy. They returned to New York in 1952.

Bob Creeley   Robert Creeley (b. 1926) had been at Harvard with MG, and at the suggestion of DL and MG had moved to Southern France in May 1951, remaining at Fontrousse when DL and MG moved to Sori in August. Creeley had been corresponding with WCW since 1950, and sent WCW's address to DL, at her request, in a letter of October 3, 1951.

❦

2. TLS-1

Nove. 13, 1951

My dear Denise Goodman:

A man should be able to react "big" to his admirers, it's due them, they do not throw their praise around carelessly. And so I always feel mean when I look into the back of my own head and see what a small figure I make to myself. I am not what they think. I am not the man I should be for THEIR sakes, they deserve something more. It is in fact the duty of the artist to assume greatness. I cannot. What a fool.

I can't believe even what I know to be the truth of my own worth. When an individual says he or she "lives" by what I exhibit I get a sudden fright. But at the same time if I myself live by certain deeds why should not others do the same? But we are so weak, what we do seems the worst futility. I am willing to go down to nothing but I don't want to feel that I am dragging anyone down with me.

Here I sit in my little hole like a toad. Thank you for your letter.

> Faithfully yours,
> W.C. Williams

9 Ridge Road
Rutherford N.J.

"Before I had met him (did not do so until '53) DL." DL's annotation on RPL
  photocopy.

Here I sit in my little hole   Although WCW had achieved wide recognition by
  1951 for his writing, his mood at this time was conditioned by the serious
  stroke he had suffered the previous March.

❦

3. TLS-1

10/24/53

Dear Denise Levertov:

Saturday, November 14th, about mid-afternoon we'd be glad to see
you and your husband, rain or shine.

Your poems in ORIGIN are well made. I like the sense of the line
which comes off well. Order, in our present disorder, without los-
ing a certain freedom of choice in our selection of the words is very
important to me. I like an understandable sequence to the words but
not an enslavement to dead sequences. That's a beginning. After
that it's just a matter of intensity of the mood, a choice of the dic-
tion that forces the pace, compels the words to obey until the reader
is astonished by the words and the intensity of the words which
show a mastery which come to mean what is put down even while
they fight against it. Writing, good writing, is still a matter of com-

pelling the words to obey. It is never easy. It must show a battle which has been difficultly won. I am interested in the sense you have of the new measures and the necessity that you feel for them. What remains to be done is simply to perfect yourself in them, without losing any of your freedom, and waiting. You can't manufacture a mood out of whole cloth but when it comes you have to be ready for it. Practice, practice, practice, is what makes the artist— and intelligence to perceive the opportunity when it arrives. Then, perfectly composed, we go to work.

We'll be glad to see you.

Sincerely yours
W. C. Williams

9 Ridge Road
Rutherford N.J.

"By the time this letter was written (Oct '53) I had met Williams more than once. The first time was with Bob Creeley & Cid Corman, I think (& with Mitch Goodman)"—note by DL filed with this letter at S. However, the comparative formality of this letter compared to WCW's next one, and Cid Corman's letter of October 9 (see Introduction), suggest that it probably predates DL and WCW's first meeting.

October 24, 1953, was DL's thirtieth birthday.

your husband   WCW had already met MG when he accompanied Cid Corman (b. 1924) on a visit to Rutherford some weeks earlier.

poems in ORIGIN   DL had been publishing in Corman's journal *Origin* since 1951. The Summer 1953 issue printed her "The Hands" and "The Rights," and the previous Spring issue her "Poem from Manhattan," "Beyond the End" (all four in *HN*), "Continuing" (in *OI*), and "Kresch's Studio." All are collected in *CEP*.

❧❧

4. TLS-1

Dear Denise:

It is extremely kind of you to interest yourself in the condition of my eyes, maybe it would be more exact to say in the condition of my reading. You have found out exactly what I want to know; the Reading Improvement Center on E.46 seems made to order and if after a few private instruction sessions I can go it under my own steam so much the better. You didn't send the name of the woman in charge but I understand that that will be forwarded later. That's wonderful!

Mrs. Williams enjoyed you and your husband as much as I did, let's make the pleasure last a long time. The next time you come out plan to bring the baby, speak to Florence about that so that the time for the visit may be advantageously arranged. Make it soon, sometime between Thanksgiving and Christmas.

You write well but you know what an advantage the poets who follow academic patters [patterns?] possess, even such relatively acceptable poets as Richard Wilbur with their regularly arranged lines, their rhymes and stanzaic forms possess. Do not underestimate it. The world they represent is not your world but it is a world that occupies the drivers seat. I admire Wilbur at his best, in such a poem as, the <u>Frog</u> for instance and poems in that vein, study him whenever you have the chance. Often he is vapor and otherwise unsatisfactory but you will have to make up your mind about him and the sooner you begin the better. A certain regularity in the actual putting of the words on the page does wonders for the poem in making it acceptable to the eye and to the mind but if [at] the cost to the interior arrangement of the words themselves (as in Wilbur, frequently with his, perhaps, unconscious inversions of the phrase) it is fatal. Today it is the death of a living line no matter what it may have done for Villon or Dante or even the Elizabethan blank versists but the solution of the difficulties involved is full of knotty problems. Nevertheless once you have embarked on writing the sort of lines which, for better or worse, have engaged you there is no drawing back. God help you.

You have our love and affection. Greet your husband for me and tell him, as he knows, that he has a fine wife.

> Sincerely
> W. C. Williams

the condition of my eyes ... my reading   WCW's vision had been affected by a second stroke in 1952, and the difficulties that it caused left him hesitant to undertake public readings of his work.

the Reading Improvement Center on E.46 ... the woman in charge   WCW attended the Yoder Reading Improvement Center, at 235 East 46th St. New York, run by Hilda W. Yoder (1903–1998), who was also at the time the Director of the Reading Clinic at the Institute of Ophthalmology, Columbia-Presbyterian Medical Center.

the baby   Nikolai Gregor (b. 1949)

Richard Wilbur ... the Frog   WCW is probably thinking of Wilbur's (b. 1921) "The Death of a Toad," in his *Ceremony* (1950).

⸙

5. *ALS-2*

Dec 5/53

Dear Denise—you have been most helpful in rooting about for the proper place for Bill to go—and he is now attending the Reading Improvement Center and feels encouraged—after only two sessions! Thanks to you.

Do plan to come out—some Wednesday or Saturday. Just now we are a bit taken up with the usual holiday madness—but with planning—we'd love to see you. How about the 16th or the 19th?

And, when you come please bring some of your poems to read to us —as well as your husband. (And youngster if you care to.)

We'll be looking forward to seeing you all again.

Sincerely—
Florence Williams

DL recalled: "I got all the info for him & he did take a course with her which he found helpful. She taught him, if he made a mistake, to stop for a moment & then go on—not to try to go back & start over. And so the reading he did at the YMHA, he did just that a few times. Her method didn't, however, help with the later trouble he had when though he cd. see the words, optically, he could not translate them into meanings & sounds" (Notes 1997).

❧

6. *TLS-1*

January 6, 1954

Dear Denise:

It's a beautiful poem, really beautiful, well deployed on the page at an even pace full of charm, as full of measure as a lovely woman walking. You write at your best so well that it makes me unhappy. What is to become of you? There is no place for you in the world I know. This poem is sad because it is like some creature that wants to tell her identity and

(An hour has passed with a call from my cousin)

I want to return to the attack. Somehow this last poem seems to come from a hidden part of your unconscious that has a particular attraction for me. Do not change it in any way but keep it in mind as my peculiar possession—whatever you do otherwise with it. It is as if a presence has passed touching the miscellaneous objects and persons that make up your composition with nothing of which does it have anything to do. After all a poem is made up not of the things of which it speaks directly but of things which it cannot identify and yet yearns to know. You have brushed the raiments of an unknown host in these lines.

The presence of poetry is an evasive thing. Don't speak again of what I have written here but forget it. But go on, as I don't need to urge you to do, writing of those things of which you have written in this poem.

If you happen to come across a new magazine just published by the english department of Washington University, St. Louis, Mo., get it, it is all about my writing. You may find it worth while. Some bookstore in the city may carry it.

Yours

W.

a beautiful poem   DL annotates on the RPL copy, "I think this was a poem called 15th St. which was in Origin but never reprinted." DL and MG lived on 15th Street in New York at this time, and again when they returned from Mexico in 1958. The poem appeared in the Summer 1954 issue of *Origin* (an issue that DL edited), but is not among the poems filed with the correspondence at B. In *CEP.*

my cousin   Probably William Wellcome, son of Irving Wellcome, WCW's uncle, See *Autobiography,* p. 303.

a new magazine   *Perspective* VI, 4 (Autumn–Winter 1953), published by Washington University, was a "William Carlos Williams Issue," but the journal had begun publication in 1947.

❦

7. *APC*

Dear Denise—You should have come back to say hello to Bill after
the reading. I was <u>not</u> watch dogging—just greeting people who
didn't want to disturb Bill while he was autographing books. I did
so want you to meet Mrs. Yoder—and looked all around for you.—
We decided that you & Mitch had not been able to get away.—Now
Bill is busy preparing a program for N.Y.U. either next week or the
week after. Hope all's well with you—Thanks for writing—
    Affectionately—F.H.W.

the reading   WCW read at the 92nd St. Y Poetry Center, New York, on Janu-
ary 27, a reading that was taped and is included in *William Carlos Williams:
The Collected Recordings,* ed. Richard Swigg (1992). FW wrote to WCW's
friend Fred Miller the next day that WCW had never read better, and had
finally learned to read slowly (Mariani, p. 681). DL wrote to her parents
the day after the reading, "It was a triumph—he was absolutely marvellous.
I was so happy to think I had had something to do with the improvement in
his reading" (S).

Mrs Yoder   Hilda W. Yoder, who had helped WCW with the reading prob-
lems caused by his stroke. See letter #4 above.

a presentation for NYU   WCW wrote to Cid Corman on February 9 that he
was to meet with "a group of N.Y.U. professors at one of their faculty club
dinners" (Mariani, p. 681).

❦

8. *TLS-2*

Dear Denise:

There is something wrong, but easily cured, with the beginning of
your first poem. Omit the first line. That aside I am as much as ever
impressed with you. There's something indescribably appealing to

me in what you write and I think appealing to anyone who reads you with attention. I'd like to be able to indicate more clearly what it is but so far it has escaped collaring. That I suspect is exactly what you want. It is a problem that eludes me.

You need a book of your closely chosen work. I think, if you thought out and selected your choice very carefully, it would be one of the most worthwhile books of the generation. It would have to be a small book squeezed up to get the gists alone of what you have to say. Much would have to be omitted. You may not be old enough yet to know your own mind for it would have to be a thoughtful, an adult book of deep feeling that would reveal you in what may not want to be revealed. I am curious to know what you are thinking— you never say. But you reveal more by your poems than can be easily deciphered and that is what draws a reader on. Perhaps you will never be able to say what you want to say. In that case you make me feel that the loss will be great.

A small closely chosen book is what I want to see packed with with the power of your selfdenials, your repressions—which would be revealed in the beauty of whatever it is a lover and a poet discovers in his heart. Things that cannot from the necessary reticenses of a sensitive person cannot be expressed but in a poem. It is the tension within ourselves that drive us to confess what is wrung from us.

Sappho must have been a powerful wench to stand what would have torn a woman apart otherwise. The tensions she must have withstood without yielding have made have made her poems forever memorable. You can say it was her fine ear that did it but she would not have been as voluble as she appears to have been without the other. Hers must have been a sound constitution in the first place. She was probably worn thin with the intensity of her longings which she refused [to] have beaten.

The dread word has been spoken.

Cut and cut again whatever you write—while you leave by your art no trace of your cutting—and the final utterance will remain packed with what you have to say. The stream does not ripple or at best go wild save by the swiftness of its flow as well as by the obstruction it encounters. But in the end you must say whatever you have to say, without honesty completely outspoken you will not succeed in moving yourself or the world.

> "And the Minotaur will devour.
> it's life against death, and
>   death wins—
> and will uproot the rocks, too, for pastime."

> "Deformed life, rather:
> the maskfaced buyers of bric-a-brac
> are the detritus only—of a
> ferocious energy—"

>   "A monster.
> Greed, is it? Alive, yes—"

> "Whose victims
> multiply quicker than it eats
> & stubbornly
>   flourish in the shadow of it."

Whoever wrote that, for it is only quoted, knew what he was doing. It can stand alone, without explanation and no matter what the connotation, and it will constitute a poem.

Pardon this screed, something set me off as it does whenever I have a letter from you. Chuck it away when you have done reading it.

Regards to your husband. Love from Floss and myself.

> Yours
> [signed] Bill
>
> William Carlos Williams

9 Ridge Road
Rutherford, N.J.

poem ... first line   DL identifies the poem on the RPL photocopy, "In Obedience" (in *OI* and *CEP*). In the typescript that DL sent WCW, now with the B letters, the poem begins "<u>Still I must tell you</u> / <u>the dread word has been spoken</u>." As subsequent letters indicate, DL accepted WCW's suggestion. DL later described the poem as "an elegy for my father" (*PW*, p. 70) – who had died the previous month, in July.

old enough yet   At this time DL was almost 31.

"And the Minotaur ... shadow of it"   DL identifies on the RPL copy: "From 'Something' (in Overland to the Islands). I've never been sure if he thought it really was quoted? – Of course the quotation marks were only to indicate the 2 speakers in the poem. DL." WCW quotes the final lines of the poem, which make up a third, separate page of the poem's typescript as he received it. WCW adds the capital letter in the first line, which ends in the typescript and the published version – "will devour them." (In *CEP*).

❦

9. *ALS-12*

> R.F.D. 1, Londonderry, Vt.
> (Back to 249 W. 15th St. N.Y. 11, Sept. 1st approx.)
> August 25th [1954]

Dear Dr. Williams,

(Or, as you signed this letter 'Bill,' may I call you that? I hate to be presumptuous, but on the other hand I get bored by my own English-style formalities – they feel stuffy sometimes) – Your letters are unlike anyone else's—this one was a great rushing wind that blew me off the ground, sent my cap sailing into the trees—I had to hold tight onto the domestic details of the afternoon and try to get my breath again—Not because your praise makes me feel over-elated [in the margin: Tho' it does too—not <u>over</u> elated, but blessed & abashed.] but because I'm afraid—afraid to disappoint you and myself. You say one must <u>know</u> what one is doing and I feel that, while I do 'know' better than X, Y, & Z, I don't know, and can't work, as you'd have me know & work. I depend so much on feeling (instinct?), on my ear, almost on luck. And you expect an intelligence of me that I either don't have or else haven't learnt how to use. You say you wonder what I'm thinking and that I never say. If I don't say it is because I'm afraid of boring you. I don't have an interesting mind. I presume I have an interesting something or I wouldn't be able to write poems; and I know some of my poems are good—I don't want to run myself down for that would only look as if I were looking for a pat on the back, & god knows I've had that—besides, it wouldn't be true, I <u>do</u> know I can write well. But it's so much a matter of luck, that's what oppresses me—the insecurity. Like those dreams people have of arriving at the office with no clothes on—I feel as if any day I might write a really bad, a ludicrous poem, and not even realize it. Only intelligence—the kind Bob Creeley has—can give security not only from a complete faux-pas like that but from—from failure to learn, to develop, to <u>know what one is doing</u>.

Mitch says I am not so stupid as I make out and why should I worry since in fact I <u>have</u> 'improved' (or developed) pretty consistently—but I go on feeling that I'm walking a tightrope.

Look—I hate to bother you but there is something I must ask you. You say I shd. cut the 1st line of one of those 2 poems—but you don't say which poem. Is it the 1st 2 lines of the poem called "In Obedience"? Or the other? I want to see how I can do it, before it gets printed – Cid has one for Origin & Bob the other for Black Mountain Review and as both are printed in Europe it takes a long time, so I'd like to get cracking on it.

Cid wants to do a book for me (in Paris) – I think he means to do a series, called Origin Editions, small, good-looking, & low-priced. If it comes off I'll try to prune, as you say. Even if I didn't it would be small though – I do so damn little. I let myself get bogged down by circumstances – i.e. by being a mother & housewife, which exasperates, defeats, & bores me most of the time. There again I guess it is a matter of intelligence – I don't organize my resources. But perhaps the answer is in your letter: "But in the end you must say whatever you have to say, without honesty completely outspoken you will not succeed in moving yourself or the world." That's the personal answer. Or part of it. And more generally there's a lot I can use in your statement and letter in Origin XII (which I've only just received).

God! I've only just – in writing this and re-reading what you wrote – only just realized how <u>much</u> of the answer for me lies in honesty. I've hidden (from myself) behind my intentions of honesty, my determination (since about 1946) not to be fanciful & rhetorical etc. etc. – and I <u>have</u> been honest in what I've written – but with what hypocrisy I have selected what I wrote! No-one knows but myself but you have discovered it. If I can only act on today's revelation (for it is really that) it will have been even much more of a red-letter day than I had thought. I've been saying for a long time, "I damn well won't write unless I have something to say, and months go by without my having anything to say because I don't have an interesting mind, I'm not intelligent, only erratically possessed," while in fact I didn't have anything I <u>chose</u> to say – perhaps for fear of revealing my boredom, bad-temper, and other things. So I stayed stuck in ditches of my own making. I take your word 'move' in that sense – 'to move yourself or others.' To move myself out of the ditch. I thought I knew this or something like it, & could certainly have learnt it from your example – but it seems to take such fortuitous conjunction of different elements to reveal anything to one in such a way that it becomes true & actually hits one.

Forgive me for writing at such length – and <u>thank you</u>.

> Love from
> Denise.

or the other "Something," see previous letter.

Cid has one The version of "In Obedience" that appeared in *Origin* included WCW's suggested revision.

a book for me ... Origin Editions the project fell through, see letter #13 below.

your statement and letter "On Measure – Statement For Cid Corman," in *Origin* 1, 12 (Spring 1954) 194–99, including a letter from WCW to Corman dated 10/3/53. The statement and letter are reprinted in *Something to Say: William Carlos Williams on Younger Poets* (New York, 1985), pp. 202–8. In both the letter and statement WCW argues, as elsewhere at this time, for verse free from outdated rhythmic models, but nevertheless with a "measure consonant with our time ... a *relatively* stable foot not a rigid one."

1946 The date of DL's first book, *The Double Image*, published in England.

❦

10. TLS-1

Aug. 30, 1954

Dear Denise:

I merely suggest for your approval that you begin the poem, In Obedience, at the second line:

The dread word has been spoken.

It strengthens the whole attack. Omit the former first line entirely—or so it would seem best to me.

I understand your whole indifference to the poem as it may at times appear to you. At times there's nothing to do but finger exercises. Maybe that's the end. You do it merely to keep supple. For what dreadful encounter? Nothing may happen, I hope it never does—but if it does, your only chance of doing some arresting writing, something that the world is really waiting for with open arms, is to be ready.

                    Love
                    Bill

the former first line   DL annotates on RPL photocopy "I did so. Forget what original 1st line was. DL."

৵৶

11. ALS-4

                              249 W. 15th St.
                              N.Y. 11, N.Y.
                              January 31st 55.

Dear Dr. & Mrs. Williams,

We got the 'Collected Essays' a couple of days ago—Mitch has had his nose in it ever since & won't relinquish it but I'll get my chance soon.

We're looking forward to hearing you (& I hope seeing you for a minute afterwards) at the Y on the 23d. By the way, do they make tape recordings of those readings? Because they certainly should, or someone shd. If no-one else is going to, we know a girl whose tape-recorder we might be able to borrow for the occasion if we could have yr. permission and that of the Y. people. And perhaps the tape cd. be presented to some library in N.Y. so that we could go & play it sometimes (no use our keeping it as we don't have a machine—besides, it shouldn't be private property.) Could you please let me know, in time?

My mother is coming over in March from England to live with us. She's almost 70. She says she's so excited she could jump out of her skin. We're busy plastering up the holes in the walls, at least, getting them plastered to the accompaniment of operatic arias by a very tiny, toothless, unfortunate, courageous & cheerful elderly plasterer who's also the current janitor. He has an epileptic (I think) son & a wife with a giant-sized crutch, & the landlady (a Greek and, or rather but, a miser,) pays him peanuts (he's Puerto Rican) so we keep taking him cups of tea, coffee, broth etc., as he works and converses, and wishing they were $10 bills. When that's over we have to get the landlady over the shock of paying for a housepainter. She has a soft corner for Mitch, fortunately.

Cid Corman almost got swept away in the Paris floods—not literally, but being in Paris causes his letters to sound as if Baedeker had been re-written by Rilke.

Mitch has been working very hard & is going to try to see if Little Brown will come across with a contract now (they did take an option before, when he had shown them only a small part of his novel).

I haven't been doing much myself but I don't feel nervously despondent, just fallow. At least I hope so.

With much love to you both from Denise.

I took Nik to Central Park after school today & we walked across the lake on the ice.

I hope you've both been well?

the Collected Essays   WCW's *Selected Essays* were published by Random House on November 5, 1954.

at the Y... recordings   WCW read at the 92nd. St. Y Poetry Center on February 23—his final reading at the Center. He had been the first poet to read there, on October 26, 1939, although of his nine appearances only the January 27, 1954, reading was recorded. At this time, the Y had begun to record more consistently the readings it staged; however in this case six days before the reading Caedmon Publishers wrote to FW asking that the performance not be recorded—in light of the company's contract with WCW for a commercial recording of his work to be issued by Caedmon later that spring. WCW accordingly wrote to the Poetry Center on February 19 that the reading should not be recorded.

my mother   Beatrice Spooner-Jones Levertoff (1883–1977). DL describes her mother's much-traveled life in "An American Poet with a Russian Name Tells About the Life of Her 100% Welsh Mother," *Poetry Wales* (Winter 1978–79), pp. 28–33, reprinted in Linda Wagner, ed., *Denise Levertov: In Her Own Province* (New York, 1979), and in *LUC* (titled "Beatrice Levertoff").

the Paris floods   In late January 1955 heavy rains raised the Seine to its highest levels for fifty years. Factories closed, some of the population was evacuated, and officials at the Louvre took emergency measures—although the river finally receded without major damage to the city.

his novel   MG's war novel, *The End of It*.

❧

12. TPC

n.d. [postmark Feb. 4 1955]

Nice of you to interest yourself in the recordings, of possible recordings, but please forget it. Sit back and enjoy the readings if you can. It is an objective for me only to know that you are in the audience.

Happy to know your mother is coming over, you must plan to bring her out, it will be a pleasure for us to meet her. I hope only that she will not be too disappointed in us.

A very charming young english poet named Paul Roche called on me last week. Love   W.C.W.

Paul Roche   poet and translator (b. 1927). A later comment by WCW on Roche suggests a parallel he had in mind with DL. In an April 1957 recommendation for Roche to the Bollingen Foundation, he asserted that Roche "has inverted the habitual routine ... of running away from America to England with all it implies" (Library of Congress, Bollingen papers).

❧

13. ALS-8

249 W. 15th St. N.Y. 11
March 23d '55.

Dear Dr. Williams,

Here are a couple of poems I thought you might like to read. The Merritt Parkway one has been printed, in Black Mountain Review, but the issue hasn't been sent out yet, indeed it seems still to be held up in the customs. The background or whatever to the one called Mrs. Cobweb is this: a lady well on in her 50's, in Detroit, whom I've never met, has through a mutual friend taken to sending me her poems to read. She has friends of the kind who go to writing courses, Breadloaf & what-not, & meet to discuss each others' work earnestly, etc. – and their work (these are also middle aged housewives, mostly, writing now that their children are grown) has a mediocre competence – pretty deadly. But this one – affectionately despised by her friends, I think – is different. Her work is completely incompetent, muddled, incoherent, crazy, but (or and) with flashes of something wonderful – a force or a radiance – The more I think of her the harder I find it to write 'advice' to her. She craves it – but what can one say. I try to show her the parts of her poems that have this quality so that she can learn to distinguish it for herself – and I suggest things she might read. I'm afraid of being clumsy with her. Anyway, the poem is about her.

It was good to see you that night at the Y. You looked well—I hope you've been feeling well. I wished Mrs. Williams had been there too. You read terrifically—but I felt mad at the audience—what a bunch of buttons. You perhaps remember that Robert Duncan came with me & Mitch. He spent quite a lot of time with us while he was in N.Y. for 2 weeks en route for Mallorca. I found his talk exciting—he's a great talker, with a loud voice that dominates any room (& he likes to be the center of attention: but not offensively, for he can listen with great attention also). He read us many unpublished poems and the talk would take off from them & come back to some image & off again—several long evenings—& I began to feel all sorts of possibilities for myself, things to do & ways to do them. I was sorry when he left. I hope he & Creeley get along. Duncan's friend Jess Collins, a painter, was tall, thin, a little bent over, and had a way of being silent (smiling) most of the time without ever making one feel he was bored, or gloomy; a beautiful gentle silence.

A friend of ours, Leland Bell, is having his first one-man show of paintings. It opened yesterday, in torrential rain. He's been painting seriously all his life (he's 32—Mitch remembers him as a boy, in Brooklyn, drawing in chalk on the sidewalk—later his family moved to Washington, but when he returned to NY at 17 or so he & Mitch met again) but has hardly ever shown even in group shows. For a long time he used to work & work on one painting—& at last destroy it in dissatisfaction. And even later he wouldn't try to have his work seen. But he has come to work with great strength & at last someone has noticed him & arranged a show. [in the margin: He has just _failed_ to get a Fulbright.] The paintings are almost all nudes, self-portraits, and portraits of his wife (who is Icelandic, & is also a very good, and neglected, painter—she's a few years older, & was beginning to have a reputation in Iceland & Scandinavia, but here she's been lost—tho' she never stops painting). They are powerful things—nothing slick, chic, or fashionable about them; intensely personal without being subjective—never sentimental, honest almost beyond what one can bear. Oh, words! I can't write about paintings. Some of them might remind one of Rouault somewhat—some perhaps of Soutine. Anyway they are really worth seeing—I know you don't go about too much, but if you <u>should</u> come to N.Y. do try to go. And perhaps you'll tell anyone you see who is interested in painting? It's at the

	HANSA GALLERY
Until	210 Central Park South
<u>April 10th</u>	(between B'way & 7th Avenue
Hours: 11–5.30 \\ Sunday: 1–5.30	
	Closed Mondays.

His name again is: Leland Bell.

I've been reading Cendrars' "Sutter's Gold"—what a story—I imagine you know it.

Mitch has sent off the finished ¾ of his novel, & a synopsis of the unwritten part, to the publisher (Little, Brown) who took an option on it a year ago—he hopes now to get a contract, perhaps $1000, to live on while he finishes it. If not he'll take it somewhere else—the agent thinks <u>someone</u> will buy it if they don't.

My mother received her visa last week & will be leaving England around April 21st. The only thing that worries me about her coming to live with us is that I'm a poor housekeeper—I'm afraid of getting on her nerves. Still, we will have the apartment painted before she arrives, so it will be like starting from scratch, & maybe I'll do better.

Cid Corman asks me to send you both his best regards. He's in Paris still, hopes to go to Greece in June. He was going to do a small book for me, first of a series to be called Origin Editions, but it has fallen through for lack of funds. However, Bob Creeley wants to do one for me instead, and perhaps that will work out, tho' not for a year I suppose. Still, by then I'll have more poems I hope. At one time, encouraged by your having said I shd. have a book, I thought of trying some of the regular publishers, but it seems silly even to try. Another possibility was that Rexroth said in a recent letter that he thought he could get Laughlin to do a book when Perspectives U.S.A. folds & he returns to New Directions—but that all sounds so far away; I guess Creeley is my best bet.

Nik is growing very tall—he'll be 6 in just over 2 months—has just learned to rollerskate (just about). On weekends he and I and some kids from downstairs go up to Central Park, the upper stretches where it's not crowded, & they scramble around on the rocks and play a vague exciting game called Sabretooth. I'm afraid his life will be stormy, he takes everything pretty hard. He remembers you both, and was upset when we went to hear you read because he couldn't go.

Forgive me for writing at such length.

With very much love—to you and to Mrs. Williams—and from Mitch too—from Denise.

Merritt Parkway one...Mrs. Cobweb   "Merritt Parkway," titled for the Connecticut thoroughfare north of New York City, appeared in the Summer 1955 issue (in *OI* and *CEP*). "Mrs. Cobweb" is in *HN* and *CEP*.

that night at the Y   WCW's reading the previous month, on February 23.

Robert Duncan   Duncan (1919–1988) by his own account had first read and admired DL's poetry in the fall of 1952, although this was their first meeting. DL describes her relationship to Duncan and the importance of his work to her—and the tensions that arose between the two poets in the early 1970s—in "Some Duncan Letters—A Memoir and a Critical Tribute" (in *NS*). Creeley returned from Mallorca to teach at Black Mountain College in July.

Jess Collins   Duncan's companion, the painter and collage artist known professionally as Jess (b. 1923) provided the illustrations for DL's third book, 5 *Poems* (1958), as well as for a number of books by Duncan.

Leland Bell   The exhibit, *Portraits and Figure Studies*, ran until April 10. Bell (1922–1991) had moved from an earlier interest in abstraction to more figurative work. He had previously shown with the Jane Street Gallery cooperative (which included Larry Rivers, Nell Blaine, and Al Kresch) before this show, which was reviewed in *Arts Digest* 29 (April 1955), p. 19, and *Art News* 54 (April 1955), p. 46. Bell went on to teach at a number of universities, was a member of the original faculty of the New York Studio School founded in 1964, exhibited regularly at the Robert Schoelkopf Gallery, and was the subject of a retrospective exhibition at the Phillips Gallery, Washington D.C., in January 1987. For his later career see Nicholas Fox Weber, *Leland Bell* (New York: Hudson Hills Press, 1986).

his wife   Louisa Matthiasdottir (b. 1917), with whom Bell sometimes later exhibited his work, and who herself went on to exhibit regularly. They had married in 1944.

HANSA GALLERY   founded as a cooperative in 1952 by sculptor and educator Richard Stankiewicz along with eleven other artists, later including George Segal and Jean Follett.

Rouault … Soutine   Both Georges Rouault (1871–1958), and Chaim Soutine (1893–1943) had been the subject of exhibitions at New York's Museum of Modern Art in the previous five years.

Sutter's Gold   Blaise Cendrars's (1887–1961) novel, *L'Or* (1925) of a Swiss fugitive and trickster who comes to the U.S. was first published in translation in 1926. In his *Autobiography* (p. 171), WCW remembered having met Cendrars in New York.

Bob Creeley wants to do one   Creeley's Divers Press did not publish a book by DL.

Rexroth   Kenneth Rexroth (1905–1982) was an early and ongoing supporter of DL's work, and included six of her poems in his *The New British Poets : An Anthology* (New York, 1949)

Laughlin … Perspectives U.S.A.   James Laughlin (1914–1997), poet, and founder of New Directions. DL had been represented in *New Directions in Prose and Poetry* 16 (1957) as well as Rexroth's 1949 anthology, published by New

Directions in the U.S. *Perspectives USA* had been funded by the Ford Foundation in 1952, and ran for four years, until its final issue, #16, in summer 1956, with various guest editors—although Laughlin was centrally involved throughout in editorial and publishing roles. As well as its U.S. edition, French, Italian, German and British volumes appeared, with the aim of putting "the culture of the United States in accurate *perspective*." Rexroth was on the Advisory Board.

꿍

14. TLS-1

April 7, 1955

Dear Denise:

Before writing you in reply to your last letter which was extremely interesting to me I have waited until I could go in and see the pictures of which you spoke. Yesterday I took in the show so that now I am able to speak to you about it. It's a good show of which I'll talk to you in a moment. Leland Bell is an artist in transition to important work. I can't say that in this show he is uniformally successful but in what I take to be his later pieces he moved me to admiration with his bold use of the primary colors. Very impressive. The pictures he painted even five years ago are grey by comparison and not interesting to me.

They are, all the paintings, figure pieces crowding the edges of the canvas. Single figures, all of them, except one which I think of as Adam & Eve, which by the way is one of the best. The style is very moving, his use of color and design, color in the design, shows him to have a lively sense of the value of <u>light</u> in a picture. That is a primary feature of all good painting, as he is showing himself more and more in his work to appreciate. The light is being permitted more and more to penetrate his vision and that presages well for him. His use of pure color, when he permits himself that privilege shows him to be a man who is emerging himself into the light of self confidence. More power to him for he has both intelligence (otherwise he would have given up long since) and emotional power.

He has to go on painting, he is only beginning to emerge from the chrysalis of uncertainty and lack of self confidence. But with these paintings, the best of them, he is just coming into his proper field and promises to make important advances. He has to give himself more room on the canvas, he has to stand more back from it and take it more confidently, he has to dare to consider a wider field – as he does in the seated figure of a man with his elbows on his knees, which is one of his best. I think but who am I? that he should paint bigger canvases – not painted so close to the eye. I'd like to meet him and his wife sometime when we come back from the coast.

You never wrote me so long a letter, so full of the small details of your life. It is characteristic of you that it took an interest in a fellow creature, an artist, to bring the best out of you. But the luminous simplicity of your style comes over from your poetry into your letters and makes you very close to me.

The poems you include in your letter have the same singleness of perception that has moved me from the first. The MERRITT PARKWAY one is particularly moving but it shows me more than ever what you are up against because that sort of composition will never be popular – even among artists. You face a hell of a future but I know you'll never change your attack. I just fear that you will become discouraged from the lack of appreciation you get – until some day, when deeply moved, you'll burst out with something which it will be worth witnessing. I hope I'll still be around, because you may need friends. Meanwhile you'll write many good poems. Work on the rhythmical organization of the poems which is not always clear, or as clear as it could be.

Love from us both.

Bill

the paintings … Adam & Eve   Some of Bell's paintings from this period, including work from this exhibition, are reproduced in *Art News* (April

1955), p. 46, and *Art News Annual* (1956), p. 89. The latter publication reproduces his *Study for Two Swedes* (1955), which may be the painting WCW has in mind here.

♨♨

15. *TLS-1*

June 28, 1955

Dear Denise:

Send my name in, I'll do my best for you. Would you consider sending a batch of your poems to Kenneth Burke, Andover, N.J. Tell him what you want and tell also that I have referred you to him. Also write to Mona Van Duyn, now at Yaddo, Saratoga Springs, N.Y. asking for her assistance. I am writing her today.

Your decision to go to Mexico strikes me as fine if you can get someone to sponsor you until you can learn the ropes. There are places in Mexico, I hear say, where you can live for next to nothing, if you are young and can take it. I shouldn't think your mother would like it though you never can tell, older people are always surprising me —and young ones as well if you come right down to it.

When your mother is sufficiently recovered to stand the trip bring her out for a meal perhaps some Sunday, we'd love to see and talk with her. She can rest here before returning. We can tell you about our trip west during the afternoon.

Go to Vermont this summer if you can possibly manage it, that state is as close to Paradise as I can think of on this earth—at least in summer for a man of my age, I'm afraid California has nothing to compare with it.

Love from us both,
Bill

send my name in   "For Guggenheim [Foundation]," annotated by DL on the RPL copy. DL applied unsuccessfully in 1956, 1959, 1960, and 1961, and was finally successful in 1962, see letter #77 below. On August 22, 1955, DL told Van Duyn – who agreed to support the request – "I'm having awful difficulty framing my plea suitably! Kenneth Rexroth whose idea it was for me to apply keeps warning me not to sound eleemosynary ... and I have no grandiose schemes for epics or anything – but I suppose I shall think of some way to say that I hope to continue as before only more so!" (Olin Library, Washington University). Other figures DL approached for Guggenheim supporting letters at various times included James Laughlin, T. S. Eliot, Herbert Read, and Jonathan Williams.

Kenneth Burke   Burke (1897–1993) wrote to WCW on July 18, 1955, complaining about the time it took him to write supporting letters: "May you rot in hell, however, for giving my name to the lady poet. I agree with you that she is good. (Above all, I liked her description of the kids getting out of school and busting loose. But it's a very subversive idea – and since she published it ["Something," in *Black Mountain Review*] I trust that she already has a dossier in the F.B.I. files.) ... my song in her behalf will be as sonorous as my cracked voice permits" (B). Burke wrote to DL on September 17, 1955, that he had told WCW he would back her application (S).

Mona Van Duyn ... Yaddo   the Yaddo Writer's Colony, where WCW spent two weeks in the summer of 1950 working on *Paterson IV*. Mona Van Duyn (b. 1921) named U.S. Poet Laureate 1992–93, was at the time the editor of *Perspective: A Quarterly of Literature*.

you never can tell   as subsequent letters indicate, Beatrice Levertoff went on to live in Mexico for more than 20 years, remaining after DL and MG had returned to New York.

our trip west   In May, accompanied by FW, WCW had been on a three week's reading tour of the West Coast.

16. *ALS-1*

Landgrove, nr. Londonderry, Vermont.
August 20th [1955]

Dear Dr. Williams,

Cid thought you would like these. I hope you've had a good summer. I haven't heard from anyone how you are. We've been up here since June—back to N.Y. next month. It's been a bad summer for work for both of us—there was no-one for Nick to play with most of the time so I was tied to him, and Mitch had a lot of hackwork to do. And it rained a lot. But a beautiful place, & constant minor compensations—birds, raccoons, bathing in a brook in the woods etc. Excuse me using a pencil, M. has gone off with my pen.

Love to you & to Mrs. Williams
from Denise.

these   According to notes on a file cover at B, this letter was accompanied by 4 poems in manuscript, and 18 leaves of carbons containing 11 poems (although in this same note the letter is misdated 1962). The poems DL enclosed probably included the three that appeared that fall in *Origin:* "An Innocent (I)," "An Innocent (II)," and "An Innocent (II) second version." A typescript of the first version of "An Innocent (II)" is filed with the B correspondence. Both versions appear in *CEP.*

❧❧

17. *TLS-1*

Sept 17, '55

Dear Denise:

Thank you for the greeting on my birthday and for the poem. Although it may not have been a productive summer I am glad to see that at the back of your head the progress still goes on. It was a happy afternoon for yesterday. The record of Creeley and Olson's reading of their poems was a thing I am glad I did not miss.

Bring your mother out to have tea with us sometime before the end of the month. Write to Floss so that we may know when to expect you.

While the weather remains as fine as it is now forget about the reading. I prefer to spend my time in the garden working on the lawn or anything that interests me than being read to. Later in the year when I will be at a loss to occupy myself I'll call on you to pinch hit for Flossie when we can perhaps take up the reading maybe of some English novel or longer poem that I have never read. But for the moment I don't want to give the time to it.

You seemed absent and lost at times yesterday among all the masculine concerns about which we were talking. We just touched the edge of something that seemed to interest you but no one seemed inclined to follow it up. For a woman, as in the case of Creeley's wife, it must be puzzling in a male world to find a way to keep the mind alive. Good luck.

With love, from

Bill

Sept 17, '55   WCW's seventy-second birthday.

the poem   Unidentified.

Creeley and Olson's reading   As letter #19 below indicates, DL later presented WCW with a copy of this recording. The 33⅓ r.p.m. disc, labelled by hand "Creeley" and "Olson" on respective sides, and made in a storefront recording facility, is now in the RPL collection. Robert Creeley recalls (letter to the editor, February 18, 1998), "As I remember, it was my idea that we do it—because I wanted Williams to hear Olson literally, whose line and all Williams seemingly had not really got as yet... I think I put it to Olson, let's make a record for him—and he agreed." DL's diary entries reveal that initially she found Olson's reading style artificial alongside Creeley's, although she changed her mind upon hearing the record again two days later at 9 Ridge Road.

Creeley's wife   Ann MacKinnon. The two were divorced in 1955 or 1956.

❧❧❧

18. TLS-1

Oct. 5, '55

Dear Denise:

You'll have to forgive me but right now it wont be convenient for me to see anyone until I can shake myself from a job of writing that has me completely tied up and can't get free from until I have finished it. I'm no good for anything until I do.

After I am free again I'll drop you a note, I'm having a hell of a time keeping up with my obligations which seem only to pile up whatever I do to prevent it. My friends will forgive me for being such a boore.

Take care of yourself and if you think I should see [it?] send it along, I'll let you have promptly my reaction to it.

Best luck
Bill

A job of writing   Probably WCW's memorial essay on Wallace Stevens, who had died on August 2, and which appeared in the January 1956 issue of *Poetry*. WCW sent an advance copy of the essay to Pound at the end of October (*Pound/Williams*, p. 296).

꧁꧂

19. *ALS-2*

249 W. 15th St. N.Y. 11. N.Y.
January 3d 1956.

Dear Bill,

We're going to Mexico the last week in January. I'd like very much to see you before we go. I have some new poems to show you, and also that record of Creeley & Olson reading—a copy of it that is. This was to have been a Xmas present but everything got muddled up—Bob borrowed the original back from the girl he'd given it to, so that I could get it copied, but then in the end he went off to Black Mountain with it by mistake. Now I have it again & will get the copy made this week. (Tomorrow, I think).

I seem much shyer, in meeting you, when a lot of other people are around, so if you have time to see me I will come alone & be more natural.

Any day at all would be O.K. for me, & any time.

Love to Mrs. Williams.

Love from Denise.
(Goodman)

꧁꧂

20. *ALS-5*

12th March [1956]
1915 Calle Florencia
Guadalajara,
Jalisco, Mexico.

Dear Bill and Floss,

That was a wonderful afternoon I had with you. I've thought of it very often in the confused weeks since then—almost 2 months. Now I'm beginning to feel clearer in the head. I was in a daze at first; partly because of the new country—so different from any place in Europe. And partly because not very long before leaving N.Y. I had fallen in love—with someone who loved me—& though I knew I was going away and would very likely never see him again, & that had to be so because of Mitch and Niki, it wasn't until I was in the plane, and thereafter, that I really <u>did</u> know it.

But I have fearful resilience; and a good marriage; so here I am, alive & kicking. (More or less.) It's sunny all day every day, there's a wonderful luxuriance of delicate flowers with an iron will to grow out of the dusty cracked ground, & we have a brand-new house on the edge of town, where the prairie begins; & cowboys and cattle & donkeys & Indians, on foot or sometimes on bicycles, with huge loads on their heads, pass by all day. Guadalajara is rather Americanized—has glossy super-markets, etc., & is growing like mad—but it has old houses too, & beautiful jumbled-up markets full of strange smells and bright colours.

We have to pay much more rent than we expected—older houses we looked at didn't have a place for Nik to play, or were too small. But we like the house, and the lower cost of food, schooling etc. will make it come out alright I think.

We heard that John Herrmann was living just outside of town in a place called Thaquepaque. I'd never been able to get hold of a copy of "What Happens" but remembering your praise in the autobiography we thought we'd go & pay our respects. We finally tracked down the house but he was out. We'll try again another day – though someone afterwards told us that he's in pretty bad shape, has been ill. We saw his little blond son, about 2½ years old, or 3 maybe.

Nik has started at the American school here. It's not a good school, but we tried out a Mexican private school first & that was worse, & at least he feels a little less strange in this one, & likes his teacher. Most of the children are Mexican & so is the teacher but tuition is in English (of sorts). In the afternoons he digs up the yard here with a friend he's made – they're making a system of canals (there's a convenient faucet on the garden wall, meant for a hose, which we don't yet have).

I don't speak much Spanish yet but have been reading some, with a dictionary.

I have a table by a window, and a view. In the foreground workmen are building a house – one of the workmen is about 10 years old, & has trouble getting up a ladder with a bucket of cement on his head & the grown men tease him, & he answers back in a little treble voice – but he seems to have a pretty good time too. In the distance are mountains.

I wish you were here in the sunshine. I love you dearly. The most.

I reread the Fall of Tenochtitlan in Mexico City where we spent a few days before coming here. We brought all our copies of your books along, except A Voyage to Pagany which got put away by mistake. Aside from you, we have Stevens' collected poems, a good deal of D. H. Lawrence, the Viking 5 vol. poetry anthology, the Golden Bough, Don Quixote – & not much else. Oh, the Cantos &

the "A.B.C. of Reading." And some books by Paul Goodman, pretty wild.

I'll put in a few poems. I feel as if I could work well here—started right in. Mitch has had to finish off a travel article so he hasn't got back to any real work yet but he mailed it yesterday & I think he'll be able to settle down to work now; he needs to get his breath & stop worrying about money.

I did write to Marianne Moore but she couldn't see me—wasn't well. Do you remember, you wanted me to go?

With love from
Denise.

The Dramamine you so thoughtfully gave me came in very useful for Nik on the trip, Floss—thank you. [added on the side of 1st page]

glossy supermarkets ... building a house ... mountains   a typescript of DL's often anthologized "A Supermarket in Guadalajara, Mexico" (in *OI* and *CEP*) is included in the B correspondence file, on which DL has added in pencil "This is just for laughs." However, the typescript probably did not accompany this letter. In a notebook at Stanford the poem, titled there "Old Mexico, New Style: Music While You Shop," is dated April 22, 1956. The house-building and mountains are part of the setting of "The Recognition" (*OI* and *CEP*), also with the B correspondence.

John Herrmann ... "What Happens"   WCW and John Herrmann (1900–1959) also author of *Summer is Ended* (New York, 1932) and *The Salesman* (New York, 1939) had begun corresponding in 1924, met soon after, and WCW published his work in *Contact* in 1932. WCW admired *What Happens* (1926), which, like WCW's own *The Great American Novel* and *Spring and All* had been published by Robert McAlmon's Contact Editions. (The novel was banned in the U.S. in 1927 as obscene.) WCW writes of Herrmann and his career in *Autobiography*, pp. 269–71, and recalls that he probably met Nathanael West through Herrmann (p. 301). Herrmann died in Guadalajara April 9, 1959, of a heart ailment. His son Juanito was born in 1952.

the Fall of Tenochtitlan   "The Destruction of Tenochtitlan," concerning the confrontation of Montezuma and Cortez, is the third chapter of WCW's history *In the American Grain* (1925).

A Voyage to Pagany   WCW's novel based upon his and FW's trip to Europe in 1924, published in 1928.

the Viking 5 vol. poetry anthology ... the A.B.C. of Reading ... Paul Goodman   *Poets of the English Language,* ed. W. H. Auden and Norman Holmes Pearson, 5 vols. (New York: Viking, 1950); Ezra Pound, *ABC of Reading* (1934). Levertov reviewed Goodman's *The Lordly Hudson: Collected Poems* in 1963 (*PW,* pp. 231–35).

a few poems   As the June 4 letter below makes clear, these included "A Clean Bare Room" (unpublished) and "The Lovers" (*HN* and *CEP,* as revised) and internal manuscript evidence suggests that "A Song" (*OI* and *CEP*) and "The Marriage" (*HN* and *CEP*) may also have been included. All are filed with the correspondence at B.

a travel article   as letters below indicate, later in the year *Atlantic Monthly* published a number of MG's travel articles.

Marianne Moore   Moore replied to DL January 20, 1956, that she was "ill," and while suggesting that DL send four or five poems, doubted that she could say "anything of value, of interest to you" (S).

✌︎

21. TLS-1

Mar. 21/56

Dear Denise:

Maybe it's just as well that you have – saved yourself to go on writing verse though you may regret it. There's no way to know what that beast of love may not do to one. Without the drive to write, and write, and write against all that may occur to stop you nothing matters. Regret is as good a goad as anything else. If you had been overwhelmed by love nothing may have come of it but satiety – unless you had gone on from love to love. Writing always better and better, more pointedly, with your eyes wider and wider open and the words cleaner, more stripped of the inessential, dared [cleared?] of every redundancy alone will give you any lasting satisfaction. It may be that women are different from men in that, they may have to strip themselves barer than men do, the history of Sappho seems to indicate it—nothing held back, absolutely nothing, complete incontinence, but the cost is exorbitant. Women can rarely do it, they are physically ruined. Not that they should not be but the cost is more than can endure. And nothing less than completely laying themselves bare is any good. They frequently do as Sappho did, is reported to have done, turn to love of individuals of their sex—though Sappho turned to a sailor at the end—presumably a young sailor. What could she do, men apparently proved impossible to her. They only wanted the one thing soon exhausted. But she was to be satisfied only with the greatest subtleties which existed only in herself. Only the putting down of the deeply felt poem in its infinite and resourceful variety could relieve her. No man could give her what she required. The poet that is not in essence a woman as well as a man can know the deocte divisions of the words can amount to anything.

But the physical satisfaction of indulging yourself or herself to the ultimate implies so many dangers that most women fail to indulge themselves enough. Better to be a writer with the imagination taking on the load.

Hope you met John Herrmann, sorry to hear he is not well. So he has a child. Good for him. I'm glad you like Guadalajara, they say it is a beautiful city. The poems are not as good as the ones you read to us last time you were here—what can we expect. Keep writing.

Yours
Bill

Sappho turned to a sailor   A reference to Sappho's legendary love of the Lesbos boatman Phaon, after whose desertion she threw herself from the Leucadian rock (see Ovid, *Heroides,* XV).

The poet ... anything   The text here reproduces what WCW typed. The *Stony Brook* printing suggested "deictic" for "deocte," although WCW may also have mistyped "divisions" at the first attempt, and started anew.

❧

22. *ALS-4*

Calle Florencia 1915
Guadalajara, Jalisco,
Mexico.
June 4th 56

Dear Bill,

Some of the poems I sent in my last letter weren't up to much as I afterwards realized. I made the mistake of sending them too soon after they were written. One of them, called A Clean Bare Room, I've scrapped entirely. And another called The Lovers I re-wrote. These I include this time I hope are better—"The Springtime" is the one I like best myself.

We met John Herrmann & his wife and see them from time to time. He was pretty sick when we first met him, and blanched-looking (after an operation for ulcers) but since then he's been away at the seaside (Pacific coast) and looks very much better. We like him a lot. He was eager to hear about you, how you were & what you were doing. I've lent him The Desert Music and Journey to Love.

It is rather suburban where we are living, a sort of Mexican West-chester, and we wanted to move to Oaxaca, which Mitch visited and liked tremendously—but we decided to wait till next year for Nik's sake—he has a good life here and a couple of real friends. Lots of Gross Motor Activity as Dr. Gesell calls it—everything that, living in an apartment in Manhattan, he's never had.

I'm reading a biography of Whitman, a new one—it's written with awful dulness by some professor but is so painstakingly detailed that there can't but be a lot of interesting information in it. And re-reading Leaves of Grass itself I came upon a wonderful poem called This Compost which I couldn't remember at all. Do you know it?

I'm helping Mitch cut chunks out of his book, by reading it over & telling him where it seems to fall flat. A lot of new ideas & realizations come up in the process. This is really his second book because what originally was the 1st part came to seem complete in itself, and the agent is trying to vend it as such—Random House has it at present. But Mitch doesn't really believe it will ever find a publisher in N.Y.—after it comes back next he may try it in London.

Cid Corman's new little book, printed in Italy where he's living, came a couple of days ago—I guess you received one also. Seems better to me on the whole than his last lot—one or two especially, really good—'The Morning Round'—'The Dying'—

Please excuse my sending you carbon copies, I had to send the 1st copies to Ferlinghetti (because I still hope that book will materialize) and I hardly ever can get at the typewriter because Mitch is always using it. He works hard. And you know, down here one senses, more than in N.Y., an envy and resentment coming at one from people (Americans, not Mexicans) because one does work. There are so many people with vague yearnings toward writing or painting, down here, but they never do anything about it, and they don't really like it when anyone else does. It's irritating because it puts one in a sort of priggish self-righteous position. But what the hell—(I do not mean Herrmann—he hasn't written for years, but he doesn't give one that feeling at all. No, it's the people who never have used themselves that are resentful).

I go swimming almost everyday. I get a terrific kick out of that—being in another element, and the sense of solitude even when there are other people in the pool, & the pleasure of using one's body.

The same thing, or not very different, I get from the ballet classes I go to. They charge me.

'Le Bateleur', title of one of the poems enclosed, is the name of the juggler in the Tarot cards.

Much love to Floss.
And to you—
from Denise.

These I include   Typescript evidence, internal references and WCW's replies suggest that the poems sent with this letter were "Tomatlan (Variations)," the revised version of "The Lovers," "Laying the Dust," "Le Bateleur" (all in *HN* and *CEP*) and "The Springtime" (*OI* and *CEP*). All filed with the B correspondence, except that WCW returned sections I–III of "Tomatlan (Variations)," see below.

his wife   Ruth Herrmann. According to WCW's account in his *Autobiography*, Herrmann met her during "the big St. Louis streetcar strike" (p. 271).

The Desert Music and Journey to Love   These volumes of WCW's poetry were published by Random House in 1954 and 1955.

a biography of Whitman   Gay Wilson Allen's *The Solitary Singer: A Critical Biography of Walt Whitman* (New York, 1955), which filled six hundred pages.

This Compost   From the "Autumn Rivulets" section of *Leaves of Grass* in the 1881 edition.

his second book   MG did not publish another novel after *The End of It*, although he published three volumes of poetry in addition to many articles, and an anthology, *The Movement Toward a New America* (New York and Philadelphia, 1970). "Mitch worked on another novel (about a man with a bookstore in NYC) for years but never finished it" (Notes 1997).

Cid Corman's new little book   *The Responses* (Origin Press, 1956)

copies to Ferlinghetti   Lawrence Ferlinghetti published DL's second book, *Here and Now*, in 1956 in his Pocket Poets series. DL and Ferlinghetti discussed in correspondence inviting WCW, or Kenneth Rexroth, to write an introduction for the book.

❧

23. TLS-1

June 13/56

Dear Denise:

"Compost" is a fine poem, thank you for calling it to my attention. From now on it occupies a niche in consciousness. But that only reinforces the main drawback for me in all of Whitman's poems, even the greatest of them and I include Compost, now that you have called it to my attention, among one [of] his most important shorter poems.

The mark of his times was on Whitman, he had rejected the older prosody but had nothing to take its place but a formlessness which has laid him open to attack on formal grounds. When you see what the young poets are writing today, Whitman might never have existed instead of founding a memorable school that should have gone on influencing the writing of poems to this day. Maybe it is best so, a great poet is strongly an individual and not to be copied but if he does not link up with the prosodic process in some way he seems to me to have lost his major opportunity.

The intellectual enlightenment that this poem signalizes is tremendous, that should be enough, you might say, to commend it to our admiration. The art of the poem must keep pace with the intellectual life of the times in which we live. A play which I saw last week which was on the verge of closing its doors because there were not enough people interested in seeing it was <u>Waiting for Godot</u>. Without qualification I find it the greatest play of a generation. It was an uproarious comedy with tragedy breaking through mostly in the acting, which was superb, but also in the idea itself. The comedy was laid on with a trowel. God it was beautifully done!

I could go on raving about that play for the rest of my life but I want to call your attention to a phenomenon of the moment in NY. That play all but failed but another play, referred to in an accompanying letter (which you can destroy), is all the vogue. You can imagine, from the title, what that is. This sort of snobbism will go on forever as long as women are desirable under their clothes. It has no relation to poetry or perhaps (we do not know) to the subtle poems of Sappho, that delightful bitch. Which brings me back to Whitman: The art of the poem requires order but in our day a new species of order, a new measure, consonant with our time. My complaint against Whitman is that he failed to realize this. He discovered nothing.

The poems you enclosed, you are right, are much better than last time. One or two of them are up to your best work. But not the last, longest one, <u>Le Bateleur</u>, which I can't see. Glad you are getting to know John Herrmann, I always liked him. Give him my love and tell him he has always occupied a special place and a distinguished place in my memory. I'd love to see him again, I hope he recovers his health completely for from all I hear he has been seriously ill.

Write again, the life you are living in Mexico sounds fascinating especially Oaxaca where you are heading. Take care of yourself. Saw some paintings of a young New Jersey painter who lives about 40 miles from us in country district about Lake Hopatcong that are quite marvellous today; thrilling work, actual records of life but NOT abstracted for a patterned to appeal to a geometric unity. Watch him, his name is Henry Niese. Love.

Bill

Whitman   The view of Whitman that WCW expresses here echoes a number of late statements he made and published on the poet, see for example *SE*, p. 339, and his "An Essay on *Leaves of Grass*" in *Leaves of Grass: One Hundred Years After* (Stanford, 1955), pp. 22–31.

Waiting for Godot   The famous play by Samuel Beckett (1906–1989) had
   opened at the John Golden Theater, W. 45th St., N.Y., on April 19, featur-
   ing Bert Lahr and E. G. Marshall, and although originally intended for a
   four week limited engagement, ran for eight weeks. Marshall later nar-
   rated the February 11, 1964, WCBS television documentary on WCW, "In
   the American Grain."

another play … accompanying letter   WCW refers to *My Fair Lady*, which had
   opened on March 15 at the Mark Hellinger Theater. In the Stanford files is
   the letter to him that WCW included from Jean Ennis, Director of Publi-
   city at Random House, in which she commented on the impossibility of
   getting tickets for the musical.

Henry Niese   The painter and environmental artist Henry Niese (b. 1924)
   just beginning his career at the time of this letter, lived in 1956 in Hack-
   ettstown, New Jersey. WCW's poem "Jersey Lyric" is based upon a litho-
   graph by Niese (in *CP2*); and see *ARI*, pp. 230–31 for WCW's statement
   on Niese for a 1957 gallery broadsheet.

❧❧

24. TLS-2

June 14/56

Dear Denise:

Your new lot of poems at their best show the ability with the words
that I have come to look for from you, the same mastery of the
rhythmic structure. At the same time it reinforces my knowledge
that poetry is is a most difficult art. It requires constant attention to
detail and a conscience that lays in wait to trip us up at the smallest
lapse from perfection. The Lovers is a beautiful piece of work.
Tomatlan, that attempts more, is also good work which I very much
like but it is not as sharply cut as I'd like to see. One word too much
in such short poems as this damages the whole effect. Without
showing it all such short poems have to be cut to the quick. One re-
dundant word overburdens the line intolerably.

The test of the artist is to be able to revise without showing a seam. In <u>The Lovers</u> you yourself state that the poem as I saw it had been revised. That proves that you have the right knowledge of what you're doing. It is often is no more than a question of knowing what to <u>cut</u>. And in the process of cutting, part of the same gesture, the new word, the insight in your own meaning will suddenly flash across your mind.

Practice, practice, practice! must be the practice of the artist. You have to write (as you must know) practically in your sleep and leap out of bed day or night when the inevitable word comes to your mind: it may never come again. You know all t[his?] but it can bear repeating, I am talking as much to myself as I am to you. All the best passages that we have ever written come to us in the flash of an —sometimes we lose them (it must be admitted) by revision, but that is a chance that has to be taken.

I return your script to show you what I would do to it—and never forget that as between writers there are no secrets. All I have is yours as far as I can make it so. I don't expect that you will agree with me. Good luck.

Best
Bill

<u>The Springtime</u> is also a well made poem.
W.

flash of an   WCW typed off of the end of the page following "an"

your script   i.e. Sections I–III of "Tomatlan (Variations)."

25. *ALS-4*

Calle Florencia 1915
Guadalajara, Jalisco,
Mexico.
June 25th [1956]

Dear Bill

Thank you <u>very</u> much for those 2 letters & for marking that poem.
I absolutely agree about the cuts—It's like someone trying to make
a 'realistic' drawing & just not seeing they've got the nose too long,
or whatever. Until someone points it out at last. Did you mean, I
wonder, to send the 4th part of the poem or not? You didn't, any-
way. Maybe you thought it was OK?

I wish I could have seen Waiting For Godot. I'm going to read it,
anyway—but that's something different. Also there's a book of 3
stories, by the same man, I've seen it here at a store which sells
French books, which we're going to buy on the strength of what
you say about "Godot." The last memorable theatre I saw was
"The Dybukk" in a little cellar-like theatre on E. 3d St somewhere,
where the stage is in the middle, audience on 2 sides, & the actors
were obliged to climb onto the stage, like boxers, from the aisles. It
was another world, and given with complete intense conviction.
And before that in 1948 in Paris, Jean-Louis Barrault's production
of Kafka, not the Castle, the other one, dramatised by Gide I think,
altho' I could understand only about ½ at most—because of the
sense of there being no slack to take up, and of things happening si-
multaneously at different levels, as in a string quartet. (And indeed
the set was built so that that was physically true).

Other plays I've seen (including Shakespeare, because played with
such embarrassment and consciousness of "playing Shakespeare")
even when I've enjoyed them, have usually seemed no more than
versions of conventional novels "acted out"—nothing specifically
theatre about them. Some sense of what it could be I've gotten from

Artaud (tho' sometimes he seems quite incoherent–or perhaps it's just that I can't keep up with him) and from that scene where the sailors dance on the moonlit deck in Moby Dick–and from "A Dream of Love"–but how I wish I could see it!

I showed John Herrmann your message and he was very pleased, & said he must write to you. But it seems he finds it just about impossible to write letters. The little boy, Juanito, was 4 the day after Nik was 7, & we went to the party. And Juanito has been over here to play several times. They like each other in spite of the age difference.

Mitch's novel was just turned down by Random House after a 9 week wait. Mitch has gone downtown to relieve his feelings. (We received the agent's letter this morning). There isn't much one could do to relieve one's feelings in Guadalajara except to drink tequila & he's not much of a drinker, or go to the movies. So I guess he went to the movies.

Lee (Leland) Bell, (that painter about whom I wrote to you & whose show you then went to see, a year or so ago,) and his wife, also a good painter, received McDowell Fellowships and are there now. I'm very pleased because they really needed something like that.

I've been reading a book on Ecology which interested me very much–the place of the predators especially. And some Fabre, insects.

We are looking forward to "Kora in Hell" which Ferlinghetti tells me will be out in October.

Love to you & Floss
from Denise.

that poem   "Tomatlan (Variations)"

3 stories ... same man   Beckett's *Trois Textes Pour Rien* (Paris, 1953)

"The Dybukk" ... E. 3d St   Shalom Ansky's *The Dybbuk*, first performed in the U.S. in 1925, was presented in a translation from the Yiddish by Henry G. Alsberg at the Fourth Street Theater, opening in October 1954.

the other one   Jean-Louis Barrault (1910–1994) perhaps best known outside France for his role as Baptiste in Marcel Carné's *Les Enfants du Paradis* (1945), resigned from the Comédie Française in 1946 and formed his own theater company. The repertory included *Le Procès de Kafka*, adapted by Barrault and André Gide from Kafka's *The Trial*.

that scene   Chapter 40 of Melville's novel, titled "Midnight, Forecastle."

"A Dream of Love"   WCW's play, first published in 1948, was performed off-Broadway for a short run in July 1949 and again at Wesleyan University in 1960. See DL's poem "A Story, A Play" (in *OI* and *CEP*).

he must write   the B files of letters to WCW contain no John Herrmann letters from the 1950s.

book on Ecology ... Fabre, insects   DL suggests (Notes 1997) probably John H. Storer's *The Web of Life: A First Book of Ecology* (New York, 1953). Jean-Henri Fabre (1823–1915) published a number of books on insect life.

"Kora in Hell"   WCW's *Kora in Hell: Improvisations* (1920) was reprinted without its original Prologue by City Lights Books in its Pocket Poets Series, but did not appear until August 1, 1957.

❧

26. TPC

n.d. [postmark Aug, 16, 1956]

Saw Mitches article on Mexico in the Atlantic. Floss read it and says it is good, she'll read it to me in the course of time. No reply yet to your last letter not because it didn't interest me, quite the opposite but just because . . Write me again when you have something to show me. I have been doing a poem now and then but nothing to show. However there is a negligible thing due to appear in New

Yorker you might like for its Calypso rhythm – if you'll agree that it comes off. Hot as – Mexico! – these days, and welcome. It was a cool July and I did not like it. Glad to hear news of John Herrmann. I hope he has regained his strength after the reported operations, now perhaps an old story. Cid Corman seems to be doing all right for himself in Italy, good luck to him.

Bill.

Mitches article MG's "Mexico" appeared in the "Pleasures and Places" section in the August 1956 issue, pp. 93–96.

a negligible thing WCW's "Puerto Rico Song" appeared in *The New Yorker*, September 14, 1957 (in *CP2*).

Cid Corman ... in Italy Corman, a Fulbright Fellow at the Sorbonne 1954–55, spent the following year as an English instructor in Matera, Italy.

〜〜

27. ALS-4

Calle Florencia 1915
Guadalajara, Jalisco, Mexico.
August 22d [1956]

Dear Bill

It certainly was good to hear from you. I hope you won't feel disappointed in Mitch's article when Floss reads it to you – the thing is, it is strictly commercial, has to be, written to a market, and he would hate anybody, and you in particular, to think of it as an attempt at a piece of genuine writing. I wish he wd. show you some of his real stuff – the only legible copy though is with Ivan von Auw, the agent. It keeps coming back from publishers with notes saying "great talent" etc. etc. "but not for us" – "however we'd be happy to see his subsequent work" etc. [note on side: And the other novel he's working on hasn't reached a legible stage.]

At the moment he is away on a trip to Guatemala, Yucatan, and the W. Indies, also for Atlantic Monthly. The Guatemalan Tourist Commission gave him a car & driver & paid all bills for a week or 10 days & he went to remote mountain villages & saw Indians proud & beautifully dressed, as they are <u>not</u> here. He'll be home in a week or so—I'm looking forward to hearing about all the other places he's seen, of which Havana seems to have been the worst and Haiti the best, after Guatemala & Yucatan.

At that point the milk boiled over.

Enclosed are a few new poems. Ferlinghetti seems about ready to send off the poems he's chosen, from what I sent him, to the printers. Jonathan Williams is also doing a book for me, and Al Kresch will do a litho for it. Jonathan put me on his list & sent that out before I even knew what he was up to, & he's going out of business (he says) after he's through with his present titles—so it's now or never—but I wish he could have waited till next year. I'm afraid of not having enough good poems for him; and I don't want to pad it. I think the Ferlinghetti book will be good, tho', and I look forward to sending you the first copy he sends me.

Tomorrow I'll go downtown to look for the New Yorker. Good!

Did you ever read Stanislavsky's "<u>An Actor Prepares</u>" and "<u>My Life in Art</u>"? The former, a very exciting book in spite of its rather wooden prose, seems to me to have so much in it that's applicable to other arts beside acting; & the latter, which I'm just reading, is full of amusing very Russian anecdotes as well as showing an interpretive artist's development step by step. I also just read "<u>The Idiot</u>" for the 1st time.

Love from
Denise.

Ivan von Auw   Ivan von Auw (1903–1991) worked for Harold Ober Associates from 1938 until his retirement in 1978. Among a number of prominent writers that he represented were Langston Hughes and Dylan Thomas.

for Atlantic Monthly   MG's essay "The West Indian Islands" appeared in the "Pleasures and Places" section of the November 1956 issue, pp. 126–30.

a few new poems   Possibly "A Supermarket in Guadalajara, Mexico," (in *OI*) "Courage," and "A Silence," (both in *HN*); all three in *CEP*, and all three with the B correspondence.

Jonathan Williams … Al Kresch … litho   Jonathan Williams (b. 1929) attended Black Mountain College in 1951 and studied with Charles Olson. As well as a writer, he is the editor, publisher, and designer of The Jargon Society, the press that published *OI*, DL's fourth book, in 1958, with a frontispiece by Albert Kresch (b. 1923).

going out of business   The press is currently located in Winston-Salem, N.C. On March 5, 1976 *The New York Times* recorded Jargon's twenty-fifth anniversary, noting that "on bad days Mr. Williams gives the impression that he would just as soon chuck the whole business." Jargon has published among others, Charles Olson, Basil Bunting, Paul Blackburn, Robert Creeley, Robert Duncan, Irving Layton, Lorine Niedecker, Stevie Smith, and Louis Zukofsky. (According to the *Times* article he turned down Allen Ginsberg's *Howl:* "He has no regrets though. 'If Jargon had published it,' he said rather glumly, 'it would have sold 300 copies.'")

❧

28. ALS-2

Florencia 1915
Guadalajara, Jalisco,
Mexico.
September 3d [1956]

Dear Bill,

Finally the September 'Atlantic' turned up with Mitch's second article – and there to our great pleasure we found your lovely poem about the turtle. I can't tell you how much I like it – everything about it.

Only I can't understand why those idiots put it in that section of the magazine. [added on side: Mitch says Charlie Morton who runs that section is the one intelligent man they have, so that accounts for it.] I've not yet found that New Yorker—but I surely will.

Mitch got back from his trip, rather tired of islands. Guatemala was the best of it—also Haiti and Guadeloupe. While he was away I found him a new workroom, as the house here he found rather noisy and distracting—that is, the sounds were all too interpretable. This room is in the house of the maid's mother—an adobe house in an alley, reached by a field-path. It's quiet, even tho' the first day he went to work there, men, women & children kept coming to the window to stare at him. But so courteously!—tiptoeing to the window, whispering very low and staring so gravely!—so that he couldn't take it amiss. And no doubt soon the novelty of a tall American with a typewriter will wear off.

Nik went back to school today—second grade. He has a nice new teacher (from Ohio, just out of college and full of enthusiasm) so we are hopeful. Last term was a mess.

Love from Denise.

Mitch's second article   "Mexico II" in the "Pleasures and Places" section, pp. 95–98.

your lovely poem   "The Turtle" (in *CP2*) is dedicated to WCW's grandson Paul, and appeared in *The Atlantic Monthly*, September 1956, in the "Accent on Living" section. DL commented when reading this poem at the 1966 92nd St. Y Tribute to WCW: "'The Turtle' demonstrates the flexibility and strength of the 3-stepped line he developed over a period of years, and which is here used in association with a content rather different from that of the majority of the poems he wrote in this form" (tape of November 20, 1966, 92nd St. Y Archives).

Charlie Morton   Charles W. Morton (1899–1967), editor and author, had edited the "Accent on Living" section since 1943.

❧❧❧

29. ALS-4

Calle Florencia 1915
Guadalajara, Jalisco, Mexico.
September 26th [1956]

Dear Bill

First—it's too late to wish you a happy birthday but I do wish you a happy year, with good health & lots of work. I didn't forget the 17th but I couldn't make up my mind whether what I'd got to send was suitable or not—i.e. whether you'd be able to read it. In the end I decided to send it anyway (with love) in the hope that if you weren't able to read it to yourself you would be able to find someone Spanish-speaking to read it to you. (Mailed separately). I was afraid you'd have to pay duty on anything other than a book.

A few days ago I had a letter from a N.Y. painter, Nell Blaine, telling me about a sort of anthology she & some other people are getting up, of poems, & reproductions of contemporary paintings, and asking me to ask you if you would contribute. The painters included are mostly good—Lee Bell, whose show you went to see after I wrote about it, for one—Hélion, Kerkam (a rather neglected older man), Albert Kresch, etc. But the poets, or at least those who are editing it, aren't much good I think; a little clique—John Ashbery, Kenneth Koch, [Frank] O'Hara—rather slick. So I don't want to be the one to ask you. However I took the liberty of sending her your address—I hope that's alright. She'd undoubtedly have gotten it from someone else anyway. Grove Press is going to publish it. I think the section of paintings will be very good.

We saw some short Lorca plays here a couple of weeks ago, very very well done by a young group, "El Caballito." Also some early renaissance things something after the style of Everyman or the Shepherd's Play; & 3 modern French plays (in Spanish)—by Tardieu, Neveux, & Ionesco. All were short, & done with wonderful crispness & freshness. They call their programs "Poesía en Voz Alta." Absolutely no ranting—(except in an arrangement by Octavio Paz of "Rappaccini's Daughter," of Hawthorne, with dreadful scenery by Leonora Carrington—the one poor item). They are the people who, if it weren't for the language barrier, damn it, could do A Dream of Love.

All this makes it sound as if our Spanish were much better than it is.

We finally got hold of Waiting for Godot, & liked it very much. But it needs to be seen—it's so hard to pace one's reading properly— rushing through what on the stage would be long pauses full of meaning.

Mitch's agent is our Godot. Right now it's 14 weeks since the book came back from one publisher & was sent to another—& not a word.

Olson's second book of the "Maximus Poems" arrived yesterday. At a glance it looks to me <u>much</u> better than the first lot, which seemed to me to need cutting. I have very varying feelings about Olson. Sometimes he seems terrific & at others incredibly bad and self-deluded. Have you read this book?

With love to Floss & to you
       from Denise.

to send it   The B correspondence contains the inscribed flyleaf, "With love from Denise. Sept. 56," of Antonio Machado's *Poesias Completas* (Madrid, 1956). DL's poem "To Antonio Machado" in *Footprints* (1972) addresses the Spanish poet (1875–1939).

Nell Blaine   Painter and printmaker Nell Blaine (1922–1996) had earlier co-authored with Koch *Prints/Nell Blaine—Poems/Kenneth Koch* (1953). The planned anthology DL discusses here did not appear.

Lee Bell, Hélion, Kerkam, Kresch Leland Bell, letter #13 above; Jean Hélion (1904–1987), Earl Kerkam (1891–1965), Albert Kresch, see letter #27 above.

a little clique John Ashbery (b. 1927), Kenneth Koch (b. 1925), Frank O'Hara (1926–1966), central figures of the "New York School" of poets.

short Lorca plays... early renaissance things Federico García Lorca (1898–1936), the subject of a 1939 essay by WCW (in *SE*). The group's repertoire included a scene from his *Así que pasen cinco años* (When five years pass), and three other short plays (*La doncella, el marinero y el estudiante, El paseo de Buster Keaton,* and *Quimera,* in addition to Juan del Encina's *Egloga IV* (Eclogue IV – a medieval pastoral play about the birth of Christ), Diego Sánchez de Badajoz's *La farsa de Santa Susaña,* written fifty years later, and the opening scene of Lope de Vega's *Peribáñez*.

Tardieu, Neveux, & Ionesco The plays in the repertoire by Jean Tardieu (1903–1995), Georges Neveux (1900–1982), and Eugène Ionesco (1912–1994) were respectively, *Oswald et Zenaïde ou les apartés, Le canari,* and *Le salon de l'automobile.* All three plays were performed in translations by Paz.

Poesía en Voz Alta The theatrical company "Poesía en Voz Alta" (Poetry Read Out Loud) was formed in 1956 by a group of artists to promote experimental theater, and allow collaborative work on sets, costumes, acting, and writing. The artists initially involved included the English author and surrealist painter Leonora Carrington (b. 1917, settled in Mexico 1942), Octavio Paz (1914–1998), Héctor Mendoza, Juan Soriano, and Juan Arreola. Paz's dramatization of Hawthorne's story, *La hija de Rappaccini,* his only play, was written for the company, and was published in the journal *Revista Mexicana de Literatura* (Sept./Oct. 1956) and in 1990 (Mexico, D.F.; Ediciones Era). The group's Mexico City base was the Teatro del Caballito on Rosales Street. For a full history of the group and its productions see Roni Unger, *Poesía en Voz Alta in the Theater of Mexico* (Columbia, MS, 1981). Unger notes that Paz himself was unhappy with Carrington's surrealistic set for the play, and also that the Company played to almost empty houses in its visit to Guadalajara's Teatro Degollado.

Olson's second book Charles Olson, *The Maximus Poems: 11–22* (Stuttgart: Jonathan Williams, 1956).

30. *ALS-2*

October 25th '56

Dear Bill

Thanks very much for sending the article. It feels very strange to get quoted. (At that point I filled my pen, and look at what strange little footmarks the blot made!) It's a very fine article and makes me feel much more 'placed' in regard to 🖋   ➤ Olson—I can see the virtues clearer, disentangled from ✍ ·   the elisions & the inessentials that, as you say, are sometimes left in. Although, even so, I don't find the poems so <u>very</u> rewarding—except, in this book, #12 (Maximus, to himself) and #19 (A Pastoral Letter) & most of 'The Song & Dance of.' But maybe it's slowness of wit in me, or ignorance, that's at fault.

"Howl" arrived a week or so ago—<u>there's</u> something I can accept unconditionally, (where I'm mistrustful of Olson, I guess, as if I felt I were going to be cheated).

John Herrmann alas is sick again—duodenal ulcers, varicose veins, hernia, & sinus trouble. I'm going to visit him in the hospital today or tomorrow. They are going to the States as soon as he can travel —probably to Houston Texas where there's a good V.A. hospital. Glad you liked the last poems I sent.

Love to Floss. Love from Denise.

the article ... to get quoted   WCW quoted the last paragraph of DL's September 26 letter in a review of Olson's *The Maximus Poems: 11–22*, with two differences ("appears" for "looks" and "varying" for "very varying"). The review was not published until 1971 (in *MAPS* 4) and is reprinted in *Something to Say: William Carlos Williams on Younger Poets* (New York, 1985), ed. James E. B. Breslin. WCW apparently originally intended the piece for *The New Republic*.

Howl   Allen Ginsberg's *Howl and Other Poems* had just been published by
  City Lights Books with a short introduction, "Howl for Carl Solomon,"
  by WCW.

the last poems   Possibly including "The Recognition," see letter #20 above.

❧❧

31. ALS-6

Florencia 1915 Guadalajara, Jalisco,
Mexico
Jan 17th [1957]

Dear Bill

First, thanks very much for subscription to "Naked Ear." That's
very kind of you. He has an extraordinary mixture of good & bad
in there, hasn't he — mostly bad — but yet it's so open & simple (like,
I've heard, the man himself) that one always feels better things may
show up. And in fact they do, e.g. Bob's poems. Bob Creeley spent
the 3 days after Xmas with us & he was describing Judson Crews
whom he likes very much.

Coming to Guadalajara & finding us gone to the coast & the house
empty, Creeley broke a window, entered, & did all the Goldilocks
things including a little laundry. When the maid's husband came to
make his daily inspection & water the lawn, there sat Bob at table
with some food & a book propped up; with his one eye & his beard
you can imagine the sensation he must have caused. He was lucky
not to have been shot for there've been robberies in the neighbour-
hood and Mexicans are gun-happy. Bob's inability to prove to
Soledad & her husband that he really was a close personal friend of
ours, & their agonies of indecision as to whether to treat him as a
guest or a bandit (they arrived at a compromise) make a comic
piece in the genre of Pirandello's "The Jar."

At the beach we ate fresh coconuts & lobsters, saw a most beautiful insouciant armadillo, swam every day, walked in the palm jungle, caught some inedible fish (tho' the water teemed with edible ones) from an unbalanced & unresponsive canoe (on the lagoon) and in addition I distinguished myself by getting a bad attack of malaria, complete with nephritis, hepatitis, & gastritis. The day before we left the bay filled up with enormous sharks, something I wouldn't have missed seeing for the world, tho' I didn't care to swim any more after that. Once or twice we swam at night—once while Bob was with us.

We were obliged to go to bed early as the candles flickered in the sea wind & hurt our eyes, so we got up in time to see the sun rise, most days.

The most delightful twinkle-footed little pigs of all colors, & their lean long-snouted medieval-looking parents, were constantly wandering through the sandy village of palm-huts & snuffing about the beach.

I have some poems to send you but Mitch has the typewriter & won't be back for another week so I'll wait till then.

The book from Ferlinghetti was to have been out by Xmas but there was some trouble about the typeface & cover so it will be a while longer.

John & Ruth Herrmann & Juanito have gone to Houston Texas where they intend to remain 6 months & then return to Mexico. John is going into the V.A. hospital there for another hernia operation, & hopes as a result to have his pension augmented. He spent a little time at the beach with Mitch before leaving. We hope, & so do they, that the complete change of scene (after 8 yrs in Mexico) will help

Ruth who has been just killing herself with drink. I went into a spin over it for a while, until I realized that no one person, least of all an emotional one like me, can do anything at all to help a person in that condition.

An image that lingers with me: — her blurred voice & tousled gray hair, her ravaged face from which glowed one beautiful eye (the other half-closed from a terrific shiner) as she recalled you coming up to her years ago at some meeting & saying, "Ah, Ruth, your <u>lovely</u> face — your <u>lovely</u> face makes it worth while having come..." And the strange dignity she retained in her degradation, in the dirty chilly kitchen among the flies & the giggling servant-girls. Somehow she pulled up when John came back from the beach & left for the States in pretty good shape. John himself aside from his poor health is O.K.

I feel ashamed to be so remote, to have given so little thought and feeling, to the Hungarian rising — but it's from the feeling of distrust one has of all the reports — not of the fact of what happened, essentially, but to the way it is used by the worst people. For example I picked up eagerly a sort of supplement to "LIFE" consisting of pictures & history of the whole affair — and dropped it without looking because however many true photographs could have been taken there's always the sickening feeling that, in that Time-Life context, they're fixed. So that the natural impulse to sympathy, indignation, etc., gets turned back on itself. All the passion and illusion of the thirties that fizzled out with the war is denied to one in the '50's because one's damned if one's going to be tricked and bamboozled. (Of course I was a child in the '30's, but I lived some of it through my sister, 9 years older than I — walked in May Day parades, held the soap-box steady in Hyde Park etc.) And then one feels ungenerous & introverted. Well, <u>Schuhmacher, bleib bei dein Last</u>, I guess.

Hope Xmas & New Years were happy for you and Floss, to whom please give my love as always.

Love—

from Denise.

Naked Ear   *The Naked Ear,* edited by Judson Crews in Taos, N.M. did not date its eleven issues, but the reference is probably to #1, which contained four poems by Creeley, "Please," "The Menu," "The Picnic," and "In a Boat Shed," in addition to poems by Wolcott Ely, Max Finstein, Hyacinthe Hill, Cerise Farallon, and Crews himself.

Bob Creeley spent the 3 days   Creeley was taking a break from teaching at a boys' school in Albuquerque, N.M., glad, he wrote WCW of the visit on January 1, 1957, to spend time with "people I love" (B).

Judson Crews   (b. 1917), based in Taos N.M. from the late 1940s, poet, editor, bookseller, and publisher of contemporary poetry. *Naked Ear* was just one of a number of little magazines he was involved with at various times.

Pirandello's The Jar   One of Luigi Pirandello's (1867–1936) one-act Sicilian plays, *La Giara* (1917), first published as a short story in 1909.

armadillo…sharks   the armadillo "<u>did</u> get into 'Come into Animal Presence'" (Notes 1997), sent to WCW September 22, 1959, while DL sent her poem "The Sharks" (in *OI* and *CEP,* and dated January 15, 1957 in DL's notebook) to WCW in March 1957; see letter #37 below.

the Hungarian rising…supplement   probably the coverage in the November 26, 1956, issue, pp. 28–37.

Schuhmacher, bleib bei dein Last   i.e., *Schuhmacher, bleib bei deinen Leisten—* "shoemaker stick with your shoeforms," or more generally "stick with what you know." Although DL recalled, "I always heard it quoted in the singular when I was a child.…My mother was given to saying it" (Notes 1997).

32. ALS-2

Florencia 1915
Guadalajara Jalisco
Mexico.
Jan. 18th [1957]

Dear Bill,

Yesterday I sent you a letter by ordinary mail—I guess this will arrive first. After I'd sent it off I received a piece of music from my adored younger brother in England (he's not really my brother but the brother of one of my best friends in England, & I was more or less part of their family for years). It's a setting of "To Waken An Old Lady" so I wrote right back to him to make another copy as I thought you would be pleased.

For years he didn't have much idea what he wanted to do & I thought he was going just to be a wonderful appreciator but not, as had seemed likely when he was a kid, any kind of creator. But now (he's 24) he seems just to be discovering himself as a composer tho' he's very diffident about it. I haven't found anyone to play it to me yet but anyway I thought you'd like to hear about it & when he sends it I hope you can get someone to sing & play it. I wd. send you my copy but then you'd have the bother of sending it back & probably the one he sends you will be more easily legible anyway.

He's one of the few people in England who without having been there has a sense of America and can read American poetry. Name is David Mitchell.

Love—

Denise.

David Mitchell   "one of my oldest, dearest friends—my friend Betty's [Rebecca Garnett, see *Life in the Forest* (1978), p. 10] kid brother...teaches music at a girl's private (elementary school) in [London]" (Notes 1997). DL's poem "The Life Around Us," in *Footprints* (1972) and "Room" in *The Freeing of the Dust* (1975) are dedicated to Mitchell (and David Hass). WCW's poem "To Waken an Old Lady" is in *CP1.*

❦

33. *TLS-1*

Jan. 23, 1957

Dear Denise:

What the hell did you have to get malaria for? Of course you were treated at once and properly with all the latest medical advice you could muster. If you had a severe case as you have indicated that you had it can take it out and may be hard to get rid of. I hope you took it seriously enough to get properly rid of it.

At that you probably had a swell time at the shore or bay or whatever you call it with Creeley. The people who take over your place for you must have been driven to distraction at sight of such a man. Lucky they didn't shoot him. He sent me a couple of poems recently, short lyrics on an enormous page which after all were very good . but so few on such a big page! Maybe that's the way to do it to give full dignity to the art. I hope so. Must be expensive.

I'm anxious to see your own book. Ferlinghetti is also I think printing my own, or reprinting them, Improvisations. Maybe they'll come out together or fail to come out together.

Thanks for your congratulations on the award, I can always use the cash.

I'm sending you under separate cover (if it ever gets there) a poem I translated from the Greek. I don't know any Greek but scouted around among my professor friends until I was satisfied that some of the classic translations I have seen were horrible then made my own transliteration. Hope you like it it may not be Sappho but I guarantee that it is in the spirit which moved her. Keep it, I'll have more copies later.

Take care of yourself.

Love

[Signature removed]

There'll be a delay of about a week in forwarding what I want you to have. Pardon. W.

[Note added by DL on RPL photocopy] "Floss—the blank square is where I cut out Bill's signature to paste it into one of his books. D."

a couple of poems *If You* (San Francisco: Porpoise Bookshop, 1956). The limited edition printing consisted of eight poems and four illustrations printed on a total of fourteen loose leaves, in a portfolio.

the award the Academy of American Poets awarded WCW a $5000 fellowship in January 1957. DL received this annual award "for distinguished poetic achievement" in 1995.

a poem WCW's translation of Sappho's "Fragment 31" was published in *Spectrum, Evergreen Review*, and in a separate broadsheet later in 1957, and also appeared in *Paterson V*, Section II (1958) (in *CP2*).

34. ALS-2

Florencia 1915
Guadalajara, Jalisco,
Mexico.
Feb 7th [1957]

Dear Bill —

— How lovely — your poem, the Sappho. Thank you very very much. I tacked it up where it gives lustre to all around it & great joy to me. It came today.

In your last letter you mentioned an award — I didn't know about it for we rarely see an American paper — what was it? Our glad congratulations anyway.

Yes I think I got good treatment for the malaria, & I'm going to get a checkup (blood-count etc.) in a week or so, also.

Glad you liked Creeley's "If You" — I did too.

It seems Allen Ginsberg is conducting a regular propaganda campaign. I saw his picture, & Jack Kerouac's, in the Feb. issue of "Mademoiselle." He has been rooting for me too, which is very kind — but I don't feel happy about it. He will damage his work surely if he puts so much energy into advertising, however generously. Or don't you think so?

I discovered 2 books by a Southern woman writer, Elizabeth Madox Roberts, who wrote with a dense, packed, and evidently true-to-herself style. ("The Time of Man" and "Black is My True Love's Hair") She died 10 years or so ago & I guess is quite well-known (perhaps to the wrong people, for the wrong reasons) but new to me.

Am sending you some poems separately. How I wish I could come to see you & Floss.

With love
from Denise.

P.S. Did you know you wrapped the poem in a Law Degree? Was it a mistake or did you want to get rid of it?

a regular propaganda campaign ... rooting for me In November 1956, Ginsberg and three companions had visited DL in Guadalajara on their way to two weeks in Mexico City. "Levertov is a good poetess, certainly," Ginsberg wrote back to Ferlinghetti, and he added a group of her poems to the manuscripts by various writers that he carried around to show to publishers, using the attention that *Howl* had brought him (see Barry Miles, *Ginsberg: A Biography* [New York, 1989], pp. 216–17).

Feb. issue Michael Grieg, "The Lively Arts in San Francisco," *Mademoiselle*, February 1957, pp. 142, 190–91.

Elizabeth Madox Roberts Elizabeth Madox Roberts (1881–1941), novelist and poet; *The Time of Man* (New York, 1926) and *Black is My Truelove's Hair* (New York, 1938) are her first and last novels, both centering upon the struggles and determination in rural surroundings of a young woman.

some poems Unidentified.

a Law Degree WCW had received an Honorary LL.D. from the University of Buffalo, now part of the SUNY system, on October 4, 1946.

❧

35. *TLS-1*

Feb. 11, 1957

Dear Denise:

Please return the case containing the law degree, I don't see so good sometimes! I thought I had emptied the damned tube before I mailed the Sappho to you. Glad you enjoyed the poem, isn't it a beauty. But I want to give that law degree to the local library.

I too feel somewhat doubtful about the authenticity of some of Allen Ginsberg's recent activities and also about his poetic abilities. But he went through a grueling time during his apprenticeship as a poet and a man and if he has survived and triumphed to any extent I want to greet him triumphantly as far as I am able. He is a Jew during an age which makes a god of advertising. He has overcome his fear of the business world, he can walk into any business office and demand recognition of the thing he represents if he can make the man he faces believe that it means MONEY! to him. He is afraid of nothing armed with that conviction. More power to him, so long as he knows that the final problem is to write well. Nothing else matters.

Elizabeth Madox Roberts broke our hearts when she died. Her books were just coming to be the sources of great enjoyment to us. I'm happy that you have discovered her. Love from us both

Bill

the local library   the Rutherford Public Library, designed in part by Edgar Williams, WCW's brother (1884–1974), which now has a rich collection of material on the poet donated by WCW, the family, and local readers and collectors.

his apprenticeship   WCW had been corresponding with Ginsberg since 1950, had written an introduction for Ginsberg's then unpublished first collection *Empty Mirror* (1952), as well as to *Howl and Other Poems,* and included three letters by Ginsberg in *Paterson.*

36. TLS-2

Feb. 11, 1957

Dear Denise:

I just mailed you a note about the certificate to be returned to me, thank you. But in the same mail with your letter telling me of my mistake in sending came Cid Corman's Origin with your poems— which you had sent me earlier in manuscript, at least the one called Tomatlan.

Reading the poems it came over me how almost impossible it is to realize what it is that goes over from a writer into a (her) poem. And how it gets there. Even the alertest reader can miss it. The poet herself (himself) might miss it . and quit trying. And yet if it is important enough to her she will never quit trying to snare the "thing" among the words. Where does it lie among the words? That is the critic's business to discover and reveal that. You do not make it easy for.

I have never forgot how you came to me out of the formalism of English verse. At first as must have been inevitable although I welcomed you I was not completely convinced, after all I wasn't completely convinced of my own position, I wanted YOU to convince ME.

Even recently I fight against accepting you unconditionally. It must always be so with a person we love and admire. It must be in the words themselves and what you find to do with them and what you have the spirit and trust to rely on the reader to find what you have put among them.

Where is it? In detail. Microscopically.

To take that poem apart or before that to view it as as a whole, what do I see? But before that where else in this issue of that magazine is there something to challenge it. I'll have to pass that one up because I have not read those poems as carefully as I have yours.

Returning to that particular poem I have spoken of, to read it gives me a sensation calm, of confidence. A countryside, a tropical jungle appears to me into which with my imagination I enter. It is done with the fewest possible words, with no straining after effect without the poet's apparent consciousness of making any effect at all.

The words used are copied direct from a vision seen, actually seen. The transition between the reader and what is being put down for him is direct, nothing extraneous has been allowed to creep in. This is a great preliminary virtue. It makes the final picture fresh as is anything seen for the first time, by a child, but let's not overemphasize that.

What, granted that, has the poet selected to use in her picture? She looking at the original picture must have selected significant details because after all she cannot sell [see?] everything and what she seizes in her imagination reveals in the first place her intelligence and her emotional range and depth. Her sight is keen, her mood relaxed.

I think the trick is done in the second stanza with the words "its silky fur brushes me". And later on "the palms shake their green breasts," . . Effortlessly, is the impression that in the instantaneous exchange that takes place in the metaphor flares as a flash in our minds.

But a poet is not to be trapped so easily (it is all a flight and an escape) an internal battle of wits and the intelligence, a man and a woman competing, wrestling for the crown of laurels, and some men and women write for cash . . Denise goodman has the ability to to bundle the whole mess up into one, balance calmly on her head, not giving herself away

"New peace shades the mind here, the jungle shadows frayed by the sea winds". The test of how the poet is going to divide her lines is the test of what she or he is.

Bill

DL read most of this letter at the New York 92nd St. Y Memorial to WCW in 1966 (see letter 92) and commented to the audience, in departing from her prepared remarks, that the letter "says a lot about his attitude as a reader, his very empathetic entry into the poem" although she did not reveal that the poem he was discussing was one of her own. Upon finishing the letter she told the audience, again leaving her prepared notes, "I needn't say how marvelous it was to get letters like that from a poet whose own work was a constant and enduring nourishment to me" (tape of November 20, 1966, 92nd St. Y Archives).

earlier ... Tomatlan   "Tomatlan (Variations)" appeared in *Origin* 1, 20 (Winter 1957), in *HN* and *CEP.* DL had sent a version with letter #22 above.

the jungle ... winds   WCW slightly misquotes the last three lines of the poem, which reads: "with jungle shadows / frayed by the / sea wind."

❦

37. TLS-1

March 17, 1957

Dear Denise:

The certificate came along in good order, I did not notice it when I sent you the Sappho poem. Many thanks.

These new poems you have sent me are in a different mood than I have ever seen in you. They are, at least, uniformly presented, without a ripple to show the feeling—like the coppery calm of that sea in which your sharks appeared. That may or may not be ominous but it is there and if I know you, which I think I do, bodes someone no good. I hope it is not you who will suffer by the reaction because reaction there will be. I enjoy you most when your words are more lumpy.

The new book, the newly printed book, has arrived from the City Lights press. I have not had time to concentrate on it as yet. When I do I'll write you again. I have been drowned with work of late answering letters principally but soon shall be able to branch out a little—I even wrote a poem this morning which I'll send you to cheer you up: not for publication till I have a chance to study it further.

Take care of yourself.

Sincerely—affectionately yours
Bill

These new poems   Typescript evidence suggests that DL had sent WCW a group of seven poems. WCW's allusion is to "The Sharks," which appeared in *OI*, as did "Illustrious Ancestors," "Broken Glass," "Action," and "Pure Products." The two other poems in the group, "The Lagoon," and "The Departure" appeared in DL's subsequent volume, *With Eyes at the Back of Our Heads*.

The new book   The copy of *Here and Now* that DL inscribed to WCW and FW is now in the B collection.

wrote a poem   Typed on the reverse of this letter is a version of "View of a Woman at Her Bath," which is substantially similar to the version that appeared in the *Evergreen Review* in the Fall 1957 issue. WCW revised the poem before it appeared in *Pictures from Brueghel* titled "Portrait of a Woman at Her Bath" (in *CP2*).

❧❧

38. *TLS-1*

n.d. [1957]

Dear Denise:

". . and all / who sit on benches in the morning" . it's a beautiful book! and that doesn't begin to say it. It's a wise book and reveals a mind with which I am in love. What is love? a fellow feeling, something we can understand and acknowledge as part of one's own being.

I haven't even finished reading the book and shall not finish reading it soon (maybe) keeping it to enjoy slowly, stretching it out to make it go slow to enjoy as I would a delicious dish of food. It is really a beautiful book. The fine points ! I am really amazed and a little in awe of you. I didn't realize you were so good though I had an intimation of it on that day in our front room when you were reading to me and I saw that you were really a poet.

> Yours
> Bill

[Note by DL added on RPL photocopy] "1957 (on pub. of 'Here & Now')."

"... and all ... morning" from lines 4 and 5 of "Jackson Square," also in *CEP.*

39. *ALS-4*

Calle Crespo #19
Oaxaca, Oax., Mexico.
August 25th [1957]

Dear Bill & Floss

It's a long time since I last wrote—you'll have just about written me off as having disappeared into the Sierra Madre.

We had a long meandering bus trip down here stopping at different places, & seeing a beautiful variety of landscape—the best being that between Mexico City & Puebla, which has not only its own riches, but the two snowy volcanoes Popocatepetl & the Sleeping Woman at its horizons. I had just received $80 for 2 poems from "Mademoiselle," so in Mexico City we had a little leeway with money & bought a whole lot of books (since Oaxaca has no American library) which was fun. I don't mean eighty dollars' worth of course! Finally we got down here to find that the house wasn't ready for us owing to a typical Mexican mishmash—that was the first week in July—now we've moved into 2 rooms & the kitchen & they're rebuilding the rest around us—it will be nice when it's finished but meanwhile the sounds (beginning at 6.30 am—continuing till sundown) of plastering, sawing, plumbing, whistling, singing, & cement-mixing (by hand) are driving us nuts, especially Mitch, and especially since the patio is almost completely obstructed by rotten beams (removed from the original structure) metal rods (to be used in the present structure) huge mudpuddles (it is the rainy season) and our landlord's family's washlines (the landlord & family are charming friends and have adopted my mother for life, which makes it almost impossible to complain, especially since all this is not the fault of anyone in particular.)

Anyway—Mitch is restless & wants to get back to New York; so he's probably going to drive up with some friends in a week & stay a couple of months. I guess we will all 3 be back next spring. The prospect of going back to N.Y. gave me the shakes as recently as a week ago but I've now realized that it is inevitable because Mitch needs it, it is his native ground & he comes to a standstill when he's away too long. For me it is rather bad than good but I'm very adjustable once I can see there's no way out. So now I'm beginning to think of the good things about a return—the chance of seeing you for one. And seeing paintings, hearing music. Nell Blaine has been painting down here & I've gotten a kick out of her work (& finding what a good person she is too, after years of mere acquaintance)—& it makes me realize how much I miss that. Here, even in Mexico City, there's nothing. The Mexican painters don't interest me, except some of the engravers. Oaxaca itself & the great archeological sites nearby I love, but somehow none of it has the impact on me that the bare dry prairie & distant mountains around Guadalajara had a year & ½ ago—bitter & almost ugly, they seemed the right place to have come at a bitter time. However once this damn house is fixed I mean to suck whatever savor is to be had from the remaining months here, if I can.

Today I discovered something odd—H. L. Davis whose poems (published by Harriet Monroe in the twenties) I'd found in an anthology & liked very much, also a book of his called 'Winds of Morning,' & to whom I'd been meaning to write to ask if he still wrote poetry, is living right here just outside Oaxaca. I haven't met him yet but am going out there in a day or 2. It was rather like finding John Herrmann, to find him living <u>here</u>—tho' I don't expect him to be such a nice person as poor John, (from whom we haven't heard recently—& in his case that's not a good sign).

The electricity just gave out (see "The Plumed Serpent," very little has changed) and there's about ¼ inch of oil left in the lamp. We were very glad to read about that Award they gave you. I hope you've both been well—has it been a good summer for you?—not that it's ended but there's a feeling here of summer visitors departing & fall beginning. I've been dyeing curtains all sorts of unexpected colors. We have a 16 year-old maid called Lydia, she has terribly bandy legs but such a nice face. The workmen's wives and families come twice a day & they all have long civilized picnics among the rubble.

With love, always, from Denise.

two poems   "The Whirlwind" and "A Supermarket in Guadalajara, Mexico" published in the January 1958 issue (in *OI* and *CEP*).

adopted my mother   Beatrice Levertoff had previously visited Oaxaca "to be a paying guest for a few weeks with a Mexican family," to work on her Spanish – a visit that lasted twenty years, until her death, and during which she "eventually became the adopted grandmother... and in many respects the mainstay of the household" ("An American Poet... Tells About the Life of Her 100% Welsh Mother," 1978); see letter #11.

his native ground   MG was born and grew up in Brooklyn, N.Y.

Nell Blaine   see letter #29 above.

H. L. Davis... Winds of Morning   Harold Lenoir Davis (1896–1960) best known for his five novels set in the American West, including *Honey in the Horn* (New York, 1935) – which won a Pulitzer Prize – and *Winds of Morning* (New York, 1952). His poems appeared in *Poetry*, edited by Monroe, on six occasions, between 1919 and 1928, winning the Levinson Prize for the 1919 appearance. DL's notebooks at Stanford indicate that she found the poems in the third edition of Monroe and Alice Corbin Henderson's *The New Poetry: An Anthology of Twentieth Century Verse in English* (New York, 1932). In the notebook DL copied out Davis's "The Valley Harvest," "Running Vines," and "Proud Riders" as well as the volume's biographical and bibliographical note on Davis. Davis lived in Oaxaca at various times from the 1930s, and from 1953–57 alternated between living in Mexico and in California – although he died while on a visit to San Antonio, Texas. His *Selected Poems* were published in 1978.

In a diary entry of Nov. 14, 1957, DL recorded: "went to San Felipe to visit H. L. Davis. Liked him – gave him my book."

The Plumed Serpent D.H. Lawrence, *The Plumed Serpent* (New York, 1926). In Chapter XV Lawrence describes the region's unreliable electricity system.

that Award see letter #33 above.

40. ALS-2

[Oaxaca, Mexico]
Sept 24th [1957]

Dear Bill,

What a lovely surprise! And just the shot in the arm I needed. Thank you very very much. When I think that authors' copies are necessarily limited, & of all the people you could choose to send them to, I am overcome. Bless you. They came yesterday & I stayed up half the night reading. So many things in the letters serve to crystallize what was already happening to me–i.e. a sudden cessation of my fear of returning to N.Y., a feeling of satiety with the slow tempo & alien remoteness of life for us in Mexico, the growing desire to get back & fight. Mitch is in N.Y. now for a few weeks, and his description of the horribly difficult lives of our friends is appalling–one young woman, a painter, married to a painter & with 2 small children (you can imagine how much time she gets to paint) tried to slit her wrists some months ago–2 others, also painters, working hard but at the price of a life of fantastic discipline (running between work & part-time jobs, shopping carefully for cheap food, etc) which cuts them off as friends, in a sense–time! time!–others desperate to SETTLE, selling out in fact–etc. etc.–you know the kind of thing. Another reported 'very nervous–dependant on the psychiatrist' (a sweet gentle creature this one)–and so it goes. And <u>yet</u> I at last (& for the first time) want to get back in there & make something of it. It's a complete volteface–only a month ago I was in tears because Mitch wanted to go back. I can't

now find the particular references in the Letters that tie in with this
—maybe there weren't any—but you will understand the connexion.
It's as though the whole time in Mexico were a long convalescence.
Of course that wasn't true at the first, when the burnt landscape we
entered then, mirrored my own feelings closely. But that intensity is
by now submerged and here, beautiful though it is, there's a soft-
ness that has begun to weary me. And the Letters clinch my new
feeling. Actually it may yet be a year before we do come back, be-
cause of various practical considerations. And when we do we'll
look hard for some place, some way, to live outside—up the Hudson
some place maybe, like near Bear Mountain. But whenever it is, it
will be very very good to see you again. Take care of yourselves.
Much love to Floss. And again, <u>thank you</u>. Love from
Denny.

Alas, I missed your birthday this year, damn it. Please accept de-
layed felicitations anyway. Love—D.

the letters   *The Selected Letters of William Carlos Williams*, ed. John C.
   Thirlwall (New York, 1957), had been published on August 27.

❧

41. ALS-10

249 W. 15th St., N.Y. 11
Feb. 9th, '58

Dear Bill & Floss,

We're back—in grimy chilly New York. Back at that ol' sink wash-
ing up it's as if the two years had never been—but they were true all
right & very full years. I'm looking forward so much to seeing you
& hope I may, if you have time to see me, about 2 weeks from now.
For my part I would come sooner than that but with Nik just get-
ting used to a new school & Mitch up to his eyes in work I can't, &
besides I want to give you time to pick a day convenient to you.

Enclosed is a little book some friends in San Francisco put out to co-incide with my reading poems at the Poetry Center there on the way back from Mexico. We spent 10 days in S.F. & had a wonderful time.

When I see you I'll bring 'Overland to the Islands'—I hope—that is, I've had an advance copy so the others shd. be here in a week or so.

Are you well & keeping reasonably warm, I wonder? I can't get used to the cold after 2 years of lovely weather. But only a few weeks to your month of March thank god & then the spring.

We got <u>Kora in Hell</u> in S.F. which is a great pleasure. So far I've only read it once through fast though for we got it just before leaving & the week & a half since we arrived in New York have been almost entirely spent in domestic matters—getting Nik started in public school (P.S.41 on Greenwich Ave.—moving now into a brand-new building on 11th St. where the old houses with wrought-iron balconies used to stand)—cleaning the apt. which the sub-tenants left pretty dirty—outfitting Nik with warm clothes—etc. etc.

I'm looking forward to seeing Mina Loy's poems when you are through with them. (Jonathan said you'd be sending them on). I have almost no idea of what they're like so if I do write anything about them it will at any rate be a completely fresh impression—but I shalln't—& indeed can't—unless I really have something to say. Hope I do!

One other thing—I can't remember if you have a tape recorder. We have a tape of my S.F. reading which I'll bring if you have, as you might like to hear part of it.

Reading a Sherwood Anderson I'd never read before—"Dark Laughter"—I feel he was very close in some ways to some of your work. He's one I go back to again & again—always with fresh excitement. In spite of the 'Sh. A. Reader' & the 'Portable Sh. A.' &

the many editions of Winesburg, I think of him as a neglected writer—so much is out of print, some of the best, & so many comments on him here & there are so snide. The way he jumps around in Time in Dark Laughter—not with boring flashback-clichés but in speculations, as the mind does,—is exciting to me—and his flexible sentences also. Those speculative re-creative looks at the past ("this is maybe how it was," is the way it happens) are much more immediate than the flashback wh. almost always seems contrived, a deliberate piece of plotting. Hope the 2d half of the book will be as good as the half I've read.

Please write when you can, & I'm looking forward very very much to seeing you both.

Love from
Denise.

a little book   *5 Poems* (San Francisco: The White Rabbit Press, 1958), six pages. Jack Spicer and Joe Dunn were the founding forces behind the press. According to Alastair Johnston in *A Bibliography of the White Rabbit Press* (Berkeley, 1985), the first ten books—including this one—were produced surreptitiously by Dunn on a press owned by his employer, Greyhound Bus Lines. The five poems were later included in *With Eyes at the Back of Our Heads* (1960). WCW's copy is inscribed "For Bill & Floss with love from Denise. February 1958."

'Overland to the Islands'   *Overland to the Islands* (Highlands, N.C.: Jonathan Williams, 1958), Jargon 19, is inscribed "For Bill & Floss with love from Denise." This inscription, and that in *5 Poems,* are recorded in Terry G. Halladay, "A Descriptive List of Books from the Library of William Carlos Williams..." *WCWR* 16.2 (Fall 1990), p. 58.

your month of March   the forces of early spring are a frequent subject in WCW's poetry.

we got Kora in Hell   i.e. the reissue by City Lights Books, published August 1, 1957.

Mina Loy's poems   At the suggestion of Kenneth Rexroth in September 1957, Jonathan Williams invited WCW and DL to contribute forewords to his reissue, with additional poems, of Mina Loy's (1882–1966) 1923 volume *Lunar Baedeker & Time-Tables* (Highlands, N.C., 1958). The 1958 edition also carried a foreword by Rexroth.

reading poems ... a tape of my S.F. reading   In *NS*, p. 209, DL describes reading at San Francisco in December 1957 as her "first public reading anywhere," arranged by Robert Duncan, who introduced her. But the introduction included in Duncan's *A Selected Prose*, ed. Robert J. Bertholf (New York, 1995), pp. 160–62, is dated 19 January 1958: and DL had arrived in San Francisco only the day before, on the 18th.

Sherwood Anderson   Although Anderson was a member of the short-lived "Amis de William Carlos Williams," organized by Ford Madox Ford in 1939, Anderson and WCW were not close personally and had little to say about each other's work.

❦

42. TLS-1

Feb. 12/58

Dear Denise:

The things that can happen in two years. I don't know how you had the courage to come back to this icy city after living in that tropical country. My disgust with this environment and the people it contains (vide this morning's headlines) turns my stomach. Well . . .

Mina Loy's <u>Lunar Baedeker</u> looks strange lying on my desk—I haven't had time to read it over, to reacquaint myself with it, as yet but I will before I forward it to you as Jonathan Williams has instructed me to. I'll get to that today.

In 2 weeks we'll be looking forward to seeing you. Call up first so that we can at least offer you a meal while we're chewing the fat.

There must be endless details you can tell us about, if you feel like it, over a bottle of wine of the best California vintage we can muster. Maybe I can show you something at this end will interest you.

Your reading in San Francisco must have interested you. How did it go? Ruth Witt-Diamant, with whom you probably stayed is a charming and alert hostess. She was very kind to us.

I have just read over J W's instructions. He says he wants a foreword by 3 of us, including myself, to ML's book. That will take some doing on my part. Wish me luck. I'm so goddamn slow with my reading and typing that it flings me on my back only to face such a job. It'll be done.

See you later meanwhile welcome home, I hope your son will accommodate without too much trouble to the changed school system.

Love
Bill

this morning's headlines   WCW may have intended his comments as a generalization, but the major domestic stories in the New York newspapers for February 12, 1958, included the highest unemployment figures for ten years, and the furor over an alleged Eisenhower Administration cover-up.

Ruth Witt-Diamant   Professor of English at San Francisco State College from 1930 to 1962, after which Witt-Diamant (d. 1987, aged 92) spent five years lecturing at various universities in Japan. She was founder and for seven years director of the Poetry Center of San Francisco, where WCW read in May 1955. She often invited the Center's prominent visitors to stay at her house on Willard Street, although MG and DL stayed with American friends they knew from Guadalajara.

43. TLS-1

Feb. 16/58

a brutal dream drenched with our lives
intemperate, open, illusory,
        to which we wake, sweating to make
substance of it, grip it, turn
its face to us, unwilling, and see the
snowflakes glitter there, and melt.

— there's nothing more to say.

        It is the despair of poetry, that there is nothing
more to say.

Bill

DL added on the RPL photocopy: "Floss — this is the letter 'Stony Brook' wd like to reproduce (along with the Y 'extracts')." For DL's correspondence with FW on printing some of WCW's letters to her, and her 92nd St. Y tribute, see letters #92 and #96 below.

The poem is identified by DL on the RPL photocopy: "'Another Journey' (Later pub. in 'With Eyes..')." WCW quotes the last six lines, and is responding to reading the poem in *5 Poems,* sent by DL with the February 9 letter. Also in *CEP.*

❧

44. ALS-2

[W. 15th St, N.Y.]
n.d [February/March? 1958]

Dear Bill & Floss,

I'm dying to come & see you but we've all been having the 'flu & I can foresee that next week, with dental appointments for Nik & a friend in hospital who must be visited, I'm not going to make it either; so meanwhile here is the book, and I'll call you at the end of next week to arrange what day I shd. come.

Also enclosed is a copy of what I wrote about Mina Loy (I'd like it back if you don't mind—when I see you). Jonathan says he's going to send me a copy of yours. I'm very proud to be appearing next to you!—and hope you'll approve of what I've written. Jonathan seems pleased. Lots of love from Denise.

the book   probably *Overland to the Islands,* unless the version of *Lunar Baedeker* that WCW refers to in his February 12 letter.

Mina Loy   WCW's comments find the earlier poems in the book "the most striking, the most brilliant of the author's compositions," while DL's praise of Loy's concision and variety is directed more at the poems as a whole, "Reading through to the last poem, and back, and through again, I hear the same true-coin ring," and suggests an influence upon Hart Crane. Both WCW and DL comment on Loy's courage and integrity as a woman and writer.

❦

45. ALS-2

249 W. 15th St
N.Y. 11, N.Y.
Friday Sept 12th [1958]

Dear Bill and Floss,

We got back from the country (Maine) on Sunday. Now we are in the throes of having this place plastered & painted—you may remember how badly needed that was! We're looking forward very much to seeing you at J. Laughlin's party on the 17th.

Hope you've had a good summer. We did. I have some new poems —a few, anyway. J.L. turned down Mitch's novel, alas. Nik had a good time at camp—learned to row like an old sailor & even to sail some, & lots of other things. We saw in

[incomplete]

This letter was probably received by the Beinecke Library incomplete, for it is marked "incomplete" on an early file cover.

J. Laughlin's party on the 17th   On September 17 James and Ann Laughlin hosted a party to celebrate WCW's 75th birthday and the publication of *Paterson V*, at the 66 East 79th Street apartment formerly owned by Laughlin's father-in-law. The party was attended by a *New Yorker* reporter, and an impressionistic account appeared in the September 27 issue.

ꙍ

46. TPC

n.d. [postmark Jan 5, 1959]

One good one, THE DOG OF ART.

You are going to have published in a brief anthology, really no more than a pamphlet, by the Academy of American poets—edited by Marie Bullock, its president, this month. You'll get it any day now. I selected the poems, hope you will be pleased . . but in view of the desperate plight of the world, not entirely due to the Russians—

Bless you, you are a poet

Bill

The Dog of Art   In *WE* and *CEP*, as are "An Ignorant Person," "At the Edge," and "The Communion"—which typescript evidence suggests were also sent with this poem.

a brief anthology   *Poetry Pilot* (January 1959). WCW's selections are loosely grouped around the theme of cats, including poems by Tram Combs, Robert Creeley, H.D., Allen Ginsberg, and Louis Zukofsky as well as DL's poem, "Scenes from the Life of the Peppertrees" (in *JL* and *CEP*).

Marie Bullock   (1911–1986), in 1934 the founder of the Academy of American Poets, and its President from 1939.

❧❧

47. ALS-4

249 W. 15th St.
Jan. 16th [1959]

Dear Bill

Thanks very much for your p.c. and for including me in the Ac. of American Poets thing, which I'm looking forward to seeing.

Glad you liked the Dog of Art.

I don't remember which were the other poems I put in.

As we burned our Xmas Tree—how it roared up the chimney!—I reread 'Burning the Xmas Greens'—Wow! What a poem that is! We're going to 'Many Loves' next Thursday. M.C. Richards (the translator of Artaud) was at the first night and was thrilled—said it made 1959 begin with a bang for her. I'm dying to see it.

It seems Olson is to read at Living Theater on the 26th, we're going to that too; should be interesting. I'm plugging away, hope to come up with something else you'll like before too long.

    Love to Floss and to you
        from Denise.

P.S. An English friend came to visit and we went up on top of the R.C.A. Building. We gazed across the Jersey Meadows to the point we thought must be Rutherford. Did you ever see N.Y. from one of the really high buildings? It's worth doing.

Burning the Xmas Greens   WCW's often anthologized poem "Burning the Christmas Greens," first published in 1944 (in *CP2*).

going to Many Loves   WCW's play, which dated from the 1940s, had opened on January 13 in New York at The Living Theatre, 530 Sixth Avenue. It ran in repertory for most of the year, with a total of 216 performances, and was revived the following season.

M.C. Richards   Mary Caroline Richards (b. 1916), freelance potter, poet, author, and teacher, translated Artaud's *Le Théâtre et son Double* for Grove Press (1958). Richards taught at Black Mountain College from 1945–56, and in 1959 was teaching part-time at City University in New York.

❦

48. ALS-8

> 249 W 15th St. N.Y. 11
> Jan 23d [1959]

Dear Bill

We went to the play last night. It was marvellous. We were completely absorbed every minute of the performance. The word "stimulating" is bandied about these days till it's a meaningless password—but this play anyway is like a swim in salt water, like a walk to the reservoir on a spring day, like a good cup of hot coffee the morning of a day one has been waiting for knowing something special is going to happen, or like a Vivaldi flute concerto on a gray gloomy day which the music transforms—well, wow, it's terrific anyway, and the performance seemed to us beautifully up to it.

There was one single thing that afterwards troubled me: the Lesbian wasn't played subtly enough (tho' Judith Malina was the best of all in all the rest of it)—I felt her approach to the girl was a bit too determined, that is, too <u>obviously</u> determined, so that all the other people—the real-estate man etc—couldn't somehow have not noticed it however self-absorbed. It needed only the least change really—i.e. in the speech where she asks 'Are there any children?' and 'Is she pretty?' If she asked the first question casually and only pricked up her ears as she asked the second, it wd. not seem as if she were buying a house only on the off chance of there being a young girl to seduce, which seems too unlikely, especially since the normal supposition wd. be that the girl wd. move away when the house was sold. Then, her expectations just casually awakened by the mention of a pretty girl, it shd. seem that on sight of her she's bewitched and begins to bewitch in turn—. It is in the presentation by the actress, not in the words, that the fault lies—the one flaw in the most exciting play and performance I've ever seen.

I feel angry tho' that such a company & theater weren't available to you long since, for perhaps you wd. have written more plays then. Are they going to do A Dream of Love? I see they don't list it, but they surely should do it.

We saw your brother sitting near us, I almost said hello, having met him briefly at your birthday party, but didn't think he would remember me.

Well—an evening like that certainly makes one feel like getting to work. I mean to go lots more times. Love to you both and thank you for having given us such an experience—Denise.

the Lesbian…Judith Malina   WCW appears to have accepted DL's point. Judith Malina (b. 1926) played the four female leads in the three playlets and frame, including the character Agnes Breen in the second playlet. DL refers to an incident in "Detail 9," and in the 1942 printing of the play the Breen character has dialogue that makes explicit her interest in the young girl. In addition, the frame characters interrupt the scene for a short exchange about the subject's 'suitability' for a play (*New Directions Number Seven 1942* [Norfolk, CT, 1942], pp. 270–71). But in the collection of WCW's plays published in 1961, the Breen character's response is left more implicit, with three lines of dialogue between her and the agent cut— including "Is she pretty?"—and most of the frame exchange cut, too (*Many Loves and Other Plays* [New York, 1961]), p. 57. DL's comment in late 1997 when asked if she knew of this revision: "No, but I'm amazed & rather pleased both at my standing up to him like that and at his taking my advice!" (Notes 1997).

A Dream of Love   First published in 1948, included in *Many Loves and Other Plays*. See letter #25 above. The Living Theater company did not mount a production of *A Dream of Love*.

your brother   Edgar Irving Williams, who was a successful New York architect.

❧❧

49. TLS-1

May 11, 1959

Dear Denise:

Come on out perhaps Saturday afternoon or maybe if you want to be with your son that day make it Thursday—or even next week if that will be more convenient for you. I hear that you are to have a conference with J. Laughlin before the next weekend as it is probably something to do with some publication of some sort, good luck with it.

As you may infer I have been somewhat slowed up recently and as the world cannot slow its pace for any individual I have been trying to acquaint myself to fit more and more into the background. A hard role for me to accept.

Did you ever hear from the Guggenheim? I can't understand those people. I give those who apply for the scholarship the best I have, and who gets the award? No one I ever heard about. It's the last time I'll ever reply to their questionnaire.

Drop me a card whenever you decide to come.

Affectionately yours
Bill

some publication   New Directions became DL's regular publisher the follow-
ing year, 1960, upon the publication of *With Eyes at the Back of Our Heads.*
James Laughlin wrote to WCW in the month following this letter, on June
22, 1959: "We are ... getting started on new books of poems by Patchen,
Denise Levertov and Gregory Corso ... Denise disapproves of the 'beats'
very strongly, and can't understand why I can like her work, which is so
disciplined and careful, and also theirs" (B).

somewhat slowed up   A further stroke, in October 1958, had left some lasting
debilitating effects on WCW's health.

the Guggenheim   WCW had forgotten perhaps that Hugh Kenner (1956) and
Marcia Nardi (1957) had been awarded Guggenheim Foundation Fellow-
ships using his name as a referee.

⤳⤳

50. TLS-1

May 14, 1959

Dear Denise:

If your note says the "Tuesday" as it seems to I cannot see you then,
nor on Wednesday. If you can come on Thursday the 21st. that will
be all right.

Glad you're coming to terms with Laughlin, he'll make you a fine
book.

If you want to put off your visit to some later date just say the word.
My head may not be very reliable now-a-days but on most days I'm

still anxious to see such a friend as you have been through the years. Bring some of your scripts that you may read to me.

Affectionately,
Bill

❦

51. ALS-2

May 23/59

Dear Denise—It was good to see you on Thursday—looking beautiful & cheery as usual—You were a tonic to us. I hope you <u>& Mitch</u> will want to come again.

There is one thing I <u>must</u> tell you about Many Loves. You asked Bill about the opening—he said it was <u>not</u> his idea. I didn't want to contradict him because it upsets him <u>so</u>. It <u>was</u> his idea and is in the published scripts as printed by New Directions Annual 1942. Get hold of it and read it.—It's sad to see a man like Bill fail—slowly—gradually—and know that there is nothing one can do.—

You are a good poet—we enjoyed so much hearing you read.—and thank you for the pleasure.

Affectionately
Floss

the opening   The specific details that FW refers to are unclear, but the opening scene of *Many Loves* underwent significant rewriting between the 1942 and 1961 printings. The revisions center around a shift in how Hubert the dramatist and Peter the play's backer, begin the opening dialogue. The play opens with the three playlets in various stages of rehearsal simultaneously, the scenery and props themselves still being prepared. In the later version the writer is "completely surprised, almost dumbstruck" to see the play's backer appear at the rehearsal, whereas in the earlier version the two "enter together" and both are "in full evening dress, even to hats." Other changes in this section include changing their initial dialogue from verse to prose, and the removal of Hubert's somewhat stilted speeches about language (which were reflective of WCW's concerns of the 1940s). The account of the actions and general choreography of rehearsal and preparation that precedes the opening dialogue is much fuller and more carefully described in the later version—since these are now being supervised to some extent by Hubert.

New Directions Annual   The play's first publication, titled *Trial Horse No. 1 (Many Loves): An Entertainment in Three Acts and Six Scenes,* in *New Directions Number Seven 1942.*

❧

52. *TLS-1*

June 26, 1959

Dear Denise:

Theodore Harris
1648 W 9th St.
Brooklyn 23, N.Y.

The guy is going away for two weeks, after he returns he will get in touch with me again.

Meanwhile he has written a piano score of the opera in addition to the full orchestral score. He has been in contact with the City Center people, I have forgot the name, and confidently expects to have a presentation of the piece in the fall. He may be a nut but there's no stopping him.

Six variations gave me much pleasure—all any of us can do is to keep working. Your new book should be worth having. I've quit writing

poems completely. The terror that overcomes me when I find myself
with nothing to do leads nowhere, don't let it happen to you.

Affectionately yours

Bill

Theodore Harris   Theodore Harris (c. 1913–1988) had agreed to write a score
for WCW's opera libretto *The First President*. Written in 1934–36, and first
published in 1936 in *The New Caravan*, WCW's libretto was originally in-
tended for the World's Fair of 1939 in Flushing, New York, where Wash-
ington's sesquicentennial was the theme. Composers WCW had discussed
the project with earlier included Tibor Serly, Virgil Thomson, and George
Antheil. As WCW's letter reveals, he and Harris hoped to have their ver-
sion of the opera performed by the City Center company. Its premiere,
however, was not until May 12, 1980, when it was performed, using the pi-
ano score, by the New Jersey State Opera's Young Artist's Program at
Kean College of New Jersey. The libretto is reprinted in *Many Loves and
Other Plays* (1961).

the name   The correspondence between WCW and Harris indicates that
Harris wrote to Julius Rudel (b. 1921). The Austrian born conductor was
General Director of the New York City Opera 1957–79.

Six Variations   This six-part poem is not with the B correspondence, although
an early, longer version of the first part, titled "The Makers" is. "Six Vari-
ations" appeared the following year in *Poetry*. In *JL* and *Poems 1960–1967*.

new book   *With Eyes at the Back of Our Heads*.

I've quit   WCW's declaration was premature. Despite increasing physical
handicaps, he was still writing poems in 1961.

53. *TLS-1*

Sept. 22, 1959

Dear Denise:

Your card which came to me on my birthday, many thanks, was re-inforced by a poem I read of yours, UNDER THE TREE, in the latest Contact. At your best you still ring the bell for me as you do in this later poem. It is hard to define what it is, not for me, I know exactly what it is but few people know that it is—the exclusive measure of the measure is that rare. When you have it you excel.

I have been ill, they carved me up early in August, I am just now be-ginning to get on my feet again, it was not a pleasant experience. In time, 2 or 3 months, I hope to recover my appetite which should lead to a substantial recovery. I haven't spoken to many people of the experience, for no particular reason except not to overburden the mails. I'm beginning to want to write again, perhaps with time the urge, the mysterious urge may return—your own perceptions lead me on.

Affectionately yours
Bill

Your card   DL sent WCW by special delivery on September 17 a hand-deco-rated, handwritten transcription of her "Come Into Animal Presence" (in *JL* and *Poems 1960–1967*), inscribed "Love and birthday greetings from Denise." Filed with the correspondence at B.

Under the Tree   published in *Contact* 3 (1959), pp. 76–77. In *WE* and *CEP.*

carved me   In New York City the previous month WCW had been success-fully operated on for a malignant tumor of the rectum.

54. ALS-4

249 W. 15th St.
N.Y. 11, N.Y.
Sept. 28th '59.

Dear Bill,

I'm so sorry to hear you've been sick & that they 'chopped' you. Wow, what remarkable stamina you have, though, bless you. I hope to see you soon but probably you aren't up to receiving company as yet so I will wait a week or two before I call Floss to find out if I may.

We have had sad news of our friend Nell Blaine, a painter whose work you may perhaps know. She has a pretty bad case of polio – is in an iron lung (in Athens – but is to be flown to U.S. in a few weeks). She's a courageous & talented young woman & a good friend – I hope so much she comes out of it alright.

Will send you more poems before long. I hope the autumn brings you poems of your own.

Much love to you & to Floss
from Denise.

Nell Blaine … polio Earlier in the year Blaine had spent several months travelling and painting in Greece, and contracted severe bulbar polio on the island of Mykonos. Following eight months in a New York hospital, including five months in an iron lung, she taught herself to paint in oils with her stronger left hand, and could draw and make watercolors with her right.

55. *TLS-1*

Dec. 31, 1959

Dear Denise:

There is about your most recent book of poems, With Eyes in the Back of our Heads, a frightening quality which marks you as a serious poet and a woman to be contended with in any discussion that has matters of art as its topic. The words, the choice of words you use is disturbing to a man. It is linked to something unknown to the male wonderfully well used . As an independent artist you hold the key to the attack, and it is an attack as long as you shall live.

The first 5 or six poems of this book challenge me so that I am glad I am not younger. It's a strange thing to have the attack come from that quarter: pure poetic excellence, quality which men have almost always reserved for themselves.

You have not always written written so excellently, as always one thinks that there is something unrevealed in such writing by a man or a woman, something deeply buried. When it is a woman that is involved the mystery deepens, it is something cryptic which the world solves by calling her a whore. But the unresolved element of superlative artistic excellence, forces a reevaluation upon us.

I am going to read these first half dozen poems — maybe more — until as an old man I have penetrated to where your secret is hid. It may be a druidic or perhaps an hebraic recrudescence but it's impressive and good for the art of poetry. You have the head for it, an impressive head which I have been long conscious of but that's only an accessory phenomenon, that curious artistic ability that flares in the words themselves is the thing to be treasured. It may at any time be lost, see that it isn't, at any cost!

I'm quitting for now.

> With love and respect
> Bill

With Eyes in the Back of Our Heads DL's inscription in WCW's copy of *With Eyes at the Back of Our Heads,* "With love to Bill & Floss from Denise. New Year 1960," is recorded in Terry G. Halladay's "A Descriptive List of Books from the Library of William Carlos Williams..." *WCWR* 16.2 (Fall 1990), p. 58.

❧❧

56. TLS-1

Jan. 28, 1960

Dear Denise:

Could you give me Jonathan Williams' N.Y. address? I have the North Carolina one but the other has escaped me in spite of his being here just yesterday. His poems and Collages have vastly excited me, they have an air about them that frees a man to go wild with a purpose. Well done. If I can get hold of his local address I'd like to write him and tell him so.

> Love
> Bill

Jonathan Williams ... his poems and Collages WCW is probably referring to Williams's *The Empire Finals at Verona* (Highlands, N.C., 1959) in which Jonathan Williams's poems are accompanied by drawings and collages by Fielding Dawson. The copy that Williams inscribed to WCW and FW (adding: "who are a fact one counts on like next spring's anemones") is dated "January 1960," and is listed in Terry G. Halladay's "A Descriptive List of Books from the Library of William Carlos Williams..." *WCWR* 16.2 (Fall 1990), p. 61.

❧❧

57. *TLS-1*

Feb. 1, 1960

Dear Denise:

Very sorry to hear of your mother-in-law's stroke, you appear to have felt very close to her. Give Mitch our sympathy. Sometimes it does not turn out as bad as it is at first thought, the first few weeks will tell the story.

Thank you for forwarding Jonathan Williams N.Y. address. Whenever you can run out to Rutherford for tea we'll be delighted to see you. No hurry but drop us a note or call up when you are coming.

> Love
> Bill

Dear Denise—I want to add my bit of regret and concern for Mrs. Goodman. I remember her with pleasure and hope so much that she will recover. No hurry about a Sunday out here. Whenever you all can make it we'll be happy to see you.—

> Our love to all. Floss.

Mrs. Goodman   Adele Goodman suffered a stroke on January 25, and died on
  February 13.

58. *TLS-1*

April 9, 1960

Dear Denise:

Bravo! the last issue of Poetry shows you to be the most accomplished practitioner of the art that we have about us. "Come into the animal presence" is accomplished work but no finer than "Map of the western part etc" You have been going ahead every time you put ink to paper. You know yourself better than anyone else can ever know you. And you have the perfect driving disposition for a poet, and I think the depth of human experience on which to draw from. It's all a mystery where it comes from, as you know yourself, no one can instruct you but gratuitous advisors will for some reason attempt to. To hell with them when they attempt to lead you into one or another camp, because I see it coming.

I just wanted to say hello and to congratulate what you have already accomplished. I know you have recently lost your mother-in-law whom you really loved and respected. What can one say? We have been to Florida but a cold wind dominated most of our stay. Take care of yourself my dear and keep on with your writing. Because we love you. And dont bother to come out to the suburbs where you can do nothing to help us find ourselves in this mystifying dilemma in which we all find ourselves.

The poet is the only one who has not lost his way, and you are a poet. We must look to you. Keep on doing what you are already doing for us.

With love
Bill

[Handwritten postscript by FW] P.S. come <u>out</u> to the suburbs when the icy winds stop blowing! Feels like snow right now—Our best to Mitch & the boy—Floss

the last issue of Poetry   The April 1960 issue of *Poetry* carried three poems by DL: "Come into Animal Presence," "Six Variations," and "A Map of the Western Part of the County of Essex in England." All three are in *JL* and *Poems 1960–1967*.

❦

59. *ALS-4*

249 W. 15th St.
N.Y.11, N.Y.
April 12 1960

Dear Bill & Floss

Your letter—such a lovely one—has come just in time to make me feel courageous about going to Boston tomorrow to read for the Harvard Advocate. With that as a talisman I ought to be able to punch 'em all in the jaw. (Metaphorically!) I'm sorry a cold wind chased you even in Florida. I had been thinking of you enjoying green & blue & gold while it snowed here. At least you did miss some of the worst weather.

I never thanked you for your letter written while Mitch's mother was still hovering between life & death. That was because I'd thought to see you & only when I was about to call you found out that you'd left for Florida. We miss her—I'll tell you some more about her when I see you, which I hope to do (with some new poems) soon after Easter. Will call you as soon as I get back from Cambridge on Monday. Lots of love—Denise.

❦

60. *TLS-1*

June 10, 1960

Dear Denise:

A week from next Sunday afternoon the 19th I am thinking of inviting 4 or 5 people out here to see a painting across the street which the artist has just shown to me just finished. It's a beauty. The guy's name is Shapiro. I don't know the first name but that doesn't matter. Flossie will give us some tea.

Will you be able to come, that is all I want to know? Mitch is invited also if he can come.

> Love
> Bill

Shapiro   Unidentified.

❦

61. ALS-1

> Red Camp, Temple, Maine
> June 13th [1960]

Dear Bill & Floss

Just walked 4 miles to the P.O. here & found your letter. Alas, we can't come! Will be down in N.Y. for a week early in July & will call you. We're in the wilds here—I'll tell you all about it when I see you. Thanks for the invitation, & lots of love from
> Denise.

❦

62. TLS-1

> Aug. 17, 1960

Dear Denise:

There is a remarkable difference in the measure of the poems you have sent me in your letter between the staid iambic and that of the American idiom. It comes out clearly when you read them aloud which is the way I hear them from Floss' reading of them. Canticle and Corazon, which are beautiful, and then in Jacobs' Ladder it suddenly it quits its gain and reverts to the former mode. Try it out and see for yourself if I am not right. The effect on the poem is disastrous.

We read your article for The Nation which is illuminating, attacks along the new concepts of the new line which we are establishing in our poems. I am happy you were able to fly to Mexico and see your mother—it shines in the imagery of your poems, you love Mexico, don't you.

I'm enclosing a short essay on the American idiom which I am broadcasting to as many people as I can reach. Do you want more copies of it and how many. Have a good time in Maine.

Love

Bill

the poems   Typescript evidence suggests that DL included along with "The Jacob's Ladder" a group titled "4 Poems from Mexico." In addition to "Canticle" and "Corazon" these included "The Weave," and "Sierra." Published along with "The Rose" as "Five Poems from Mexico" in *JL* and *Poems 1960–1967*.

your article   no article by DL appeared in *The Nation* in 1960. WCW is probably responding to the typescript of an unpublished essay titled "The Poem as Counterforce: Responsibilities & Possibilities" (c. 1960), filed with the correspondence at B. A number of its elements appear in DL's 1965 essay, "Some Notes on Organic Form" (in *PW*).

a short essay   WCW had many mimeographed copies of this essay printed, sending them to numerous correspondents and journals. The essay, printed in a number of places, including *New Directions 17* (1961), argues that American speech should be the measure of American poetry, as against what WCW sees as the inappropriate prestige given to outmoded conventions that are associated with British usage. On the back of one of the five copies with the correspondence at Stanford, WCW has typed "May you profit by this" and signed "Bill."

⁕

63. ALS-11

249 W. 15th St.
N.Y. 11, N.Y.
September 21st [1960]

Dear Bill & Floss,

I have been incredibly sloppy about all letters this summer—please forgive my rudeness in not writing back sooner to thank you for 'The American Idiom' & to answer your remarks on my recent poems. By way of excuse, the truth is I was having such a good time out of doors in Maine, swimming & swimming and walking & just looking, that I hated to spend any time indoors in my rather stuffy little study there—also, at the last, we were in a state of paralyzing tension over the question of whether we should put every penny we have (& it's the first, fortuitous, & perhaps last time we had the extra money at all) on an old farmhouse. Well, we've done it—at least I think so—negotiations were to have been completed a couple of days ago, Mitch having remained up there for that purpose—but I haven't heard yet.

Now, about 'The American Idiom.' I agree that there are very many young writers (older ones aren't likely to change anyway) who need to have this said to them because they start out writing in a borrowed 'literary' style that doesn't have roots in their own life & doesn't correspond to how they feel and how they talk. Also I agree that there is marvellous poetry in common speech, painful heartbreaking human poetry only to be heard & cherished if the poet hears and frees it—your life's work evidences that.

But—for me personally, I cannot put the idea of "American idiom" first. For you it has always been a focus, almost a mission. But each person must know their own needs. My need and desire is in each poem to find the tone and measure of what I feel, whether the language, word by word or measure by measure, strikes the reader as 'American' or not. That poem you were distressed by, 'The Jacob's Ladder,' has to be the way it is because it sounds the way I think and feel about it, just as close as I can make it. My shaking up of its structure into something else would be a betrayal of what I know I must do. You must take into consideration that I grew up not in an American, and not in an English, but a European atmosphere; my father was naturalized in Eng. only around the time I was born—his background was Jewish, Russian, Central European—and my mother, herself proudly Welsh; had lived in Poland, Germany, & Denmark etc all the years between 1910 & 1923. And then, when I came to the U.S., I was already 24 years old—so tho' I was very impressionable, good melting-pot material, the American idiom is an acquired language for me. Certainly I am an American poet, if anything—I know I am not an English one—nevertheless I feel the great European poets 'belong to me' as an inheritance too. It may perhaps not be a good thing to be without deep local roots, to be at home everywhere & nowhere, but if one's life has made one be such a person, & one is a poet by natural aptitude & constitution, one surely must accept it: for instance, my daily speech is not purely American—I'm adaptable & often modify it to fit with whoever I'm with, but in speaking to Mitch or to myself my vocabulary is a mixture of different elements—more American than anything else but still not standard American so to speak—if such a thing existed, which of course it doesn't. And I believe fervently that the poet's first obligation is to his own voice—to find it and use it. And one's 'voice' does not speak only in the often slipshod imprecise vocabulary with which one buys the groceries but with all the resources of one's life whatever they may be, no matter whether they are 'American' or of other cultures, so long as they are truly one's own & not faked.

Add to this the fact that 'The Jacob's Ladder' was written in a church in Mexico (begun there, at least, looking at a primitive painting).

Also, it is most certainly not in iambics. When I come to see you (soon, I hope) I'll read it to you & if you are still interested we'll battle it out.

Glad you liked some of the other poems and hope you don't feel I am defecting from all you hold dear—your own work remains as rich and necessary to me as it has since I first began to read it 13 years ago but I cannot simply go along with all you say about the American Language [added at bottom of page: Even though I think it is healthy for those who grow up entirely <u>in</u> that language to realize it & use it.] and I think you have to grant that I'm a special case anyway—I'm a later naturalized, second-class citizen, not an all-American girl, & I'm darned if I'm going to pretend to be anything else or throw out what other cultural influences I have in my system, whatever <u>anyone</u> says.

Much love always Denise

P.S. Gee, just realized as I dated this letter that your birthday was on Saturday. Please accept my wishes for a year of good health and of many poems and joys. Love—

                              D.

Please save me some copies of 'The American Idiom' because I have some college reading dates & can give them away to students.

'The American Idiom'   DL wrote to Mary Ellen Solt the following month (see note to October 8 letter below) of WCW's essay: "I feel Bill is beating, not a dead, but a vigorously trotting horse at this point, because so many poets <u>have</u> long since accepted the 'American idiom' as their medium. No, what is needed is not <u>that</u> emphasis, but to encourage a more craftsmanlike <u>use</u> of it! Bill's various notes on <u>measure</u> have many times more value than this repetitive (alas, muddled) release of his which will only do him harm I'm afraid," quoted in Mary Ellen Solt, "The American Idiom," 9.1–2 (Fall 1983), pp. 120, 124.

a <u>European</u> atmosphere   DL describes the background of her parents and her early life in England in *Tesserae: Memories and Suppositions* (New York, 1995).

a church in Mexico   "The church of Santo Domingo, in Oaxaca. It has 2 tiers of paintings (frescos) high on the walls of the nave. The lower...are of N.T. subjects & the upper are of O.T. subjects & are somewhat more primitive. Among the latter is Jacob's Dream" (Notes 1997).

naturalized   DL became a U.S. citizen in 1955.

some copies   WCW may have sent additional copies. As noted above, the Stanford correspondence includes four extra copies of the essay.

❧❧

64. TLS-1

Sept. 22/60

Dear Denise:

Thanks for your explicit letter about your family history and your life after coming to America as it applies to your language, it is very enlightening. So our language has been made up, there is one thing that draws us together: the spoken language.

Congratulations on your purchasing for yourselves a home. May you have much happiness from living in it. Come see us when you have the time.

Love
Bill

❧❧

65. *ALS-4*

Oct 8th [1960]

Dear Bill & Floss,

I'm writing this in the bus on the way back from reading at Bard. Stayed with Ted Weiss & had a good time—tho' I know I read too fast, darn it, & didn't space the poems out enough.

We're in the process of moving. Left the apartment yesterday with every drawer hanging open, boxes all over the place, packed and half-packed—trunks with clothes lolloping out of their open mouths, etc. It is fatiguing but also exhilarating.

I found Mary Ellen Solt's approach (in her letter) a little Germanic & pedestrian, in other words academic—the prose about poetry of a non-practitioner. The point gets lost among so many words.

Here is a poem you may like—I hope.

I want to see you both. This household removal—I have to get that over first.

Bus is close to Rutherford now—wish I cd jump off & come over—but back to the boxes—

With love—

Denise

After the 13th of October: 277 Greenwich St N Y 7

Ted Weiss   The poet Ted Weiss (b. 1916), along with his wife Renee editors of *The Quarterly Review of Literature*, then based at Bard College, N.Y.

Mary Ellen Solt's approach   Mary Ellen Solt (b. 1920), a freelance writer, had taken a summer course at Indiana University with R. P. Blackmur in 1958, and had written a paper on WCW's poetics. When, at the suggestion of Blackmur, she sent it to WCW, he was enthusiastic about her approach and later invited her to Rutherford. See Solt's "William Carlos Williams: Poems in the American Idiom," *Folio* XXV.1 (Winter 1960), pp. 17, 20–27.

a non-practitioner   DL would not have known that Solt had been writing poems for some years, although the interest in Concrete Poetry at the center of her mature work did not develop until 1962. She later published *Flowers in Concrete* (Bloomington, IN, 1966), the anthology *Concrete Poetry: A World View* (1968), and has contributed poems to a number of anthologies and periodicals. She joined the faculty at Indiana in 1970, retiring in 1991.

a poem   Possibly "The Thread," dated in one draft August 13, 1960. The poem is in *JL* and *Poems 1960–1967*, and filed with the correspondence at B.

ᔛᔛ

66. *TLS-1*

Oct. 10/60

Dear Denise:

A very good poem, this last, true in its composition to the best that you have learned in this country since leaving England, beautifully done, pared to the bone, not a phrase redundant. Thank you.

Mary [Ellen] Solt I am sorry to say is faulty in her thinking, her prose cannot hold an edge, not thought through; she talks too much. I agree with you, I was shocked when I heard her read but I can't do anything about it. Let her have it if you ever get the chance because the girl is right in her premises but doesn't know how to put it over to become effective.

When you have moved to your new apartment let us know, plan to come out and read to me. Cal Lowell was here on Saturday, he's a wonderful guy and one of my best friends. He read me some of his translations he is doing from the French classics and Baudelaire, it's amazing how the American idiom has penetrated his diction. I didn't say a word but he's good.

I worked on a new poem over the weekend. Came out quite well I think. Show it to you as soon as I get the chance to copy it.

Bill.

Cal Lowell ... his translations In *The Harvard Advocate* (Nov. 1962) WCW reviewed Robert Lowell's (1917–1977) *Imitations* (New York, 1961), in which these poems appear.

a new poem Probably "Jersey Lyric," in *CP2*, based on a lithograph by Henry Niese.

❧❧

67. TLS-1

Nov. 6/60

Dear Denise:

Our talk yesterday afternoon was very important and rewarding to me, it put me straight on a subject on which I was too lazy to have made up my mind, a subject of utmost importance to me.

It had directly to do with that second poem which I had slighted but which I now see is one of the best you have ever written, employing the very understanding I am most eager to see in a poet—his relationship with the art itself rather than any topical matter which curses even our most promising artist.

The measured way in which you handled your material of the Jacob

Ladder incident until the very scraping of the angels' wings upon the stone makes me cringe with embarrassment that I should have missed it in the first place.

The clean handling of the language is brilliantly deployed – you are an artist who it does my heart good to have seen in action. That's not half of it. Your criticism of my own short comings is noted. I'll pay attention to what you say.

Love

Bill

[Note added by DL on RPL photocopy] "Can't _imagine_ what this meant. Maybe that in reading, he ignored his own beautifully structured line-breaks. DL"

that second poem   "The Jacob's Ladder": see letters #62 and #63 above.

ᘛᘚ

68. ALS-2

277 Greenwich St N.Y. 7
Nov 11th 1960

Dear Bill

Thank you for your lovely letter. I am thinking about that last poem I read to you, about taking the clean clothes off the line in the dark, etc. – you probably don't remember because it was so confused – and about how I can tighten it up, as you said, without losing any sense of speed & wildness it may have.

I had, as always, a wonderful visit with you & Floss. The chrysanthemums are still living. I meant to go to the Paterson reading but by 8pm on Monday I was so tired, I was afraid I was coming down with flu or something, [at bottom of page: I wasn't – just tired.] so I stayed home. Hope it was good. When I next see you I'd love to hear whether Betty Kray ever came to, and realized she hadn't invited you, or what.

With love—

Denise.

that last poem   "From the Roof" in *JL* and *Poems 1960–1967.*

the Paterson reading   On November 7, 1960, the Poetry Center at the 92nd St. Y. staged a reading from *Paterson*, Book I. The reading was introduced by Robert Lowell, and the poetry read by Lowell, Arthur Luce Klein, Kevin McCarthy, Judith Malina, Kenneth Koch, and Talley Beatty.

Betty Kray   Elizabeth Kray (1916–1987), became Director of the 92nd. St. Y Poetry Center in 1954, and from 1963 to 1981 was executive director of the Academy of American Poets.

❧❧

69. ALS-2

277 Greenwich St N.Y.7
Nov 18th 1960

Dear Bill & Floss

I've a poem I think I might try on the Ladies Home Journal as you suggested. Could you please let me know the name of the poetry editor there? And may I say you suggested that I send her something?

Had a good visit to U. of Pittsburgh. It's quite an interesting city, full of conflict and contrasts. It's a good thing I didn't stay with Jay's mother because lots of the students are the children or grandchildren of steelworkers to whom the name of Laughlin is mud. The small yellow chrysanthemums lasted until today! Love—

Denise.

a poem   DL's notebooks at Stanford indicate that "The Fountain" was the poem sent to *Ladies' Home Journal*. The poem is dated there "Nov 1960" (in *JL* and *Poems 1960–1967*); it had no periodical publication, and the journal published no poem by DL.

Jay's mother   James Laughlin's mother, Marjory Rea Laughlin (1884–1966).

steelworkers   The Laughlin family had been partners since the mid-nineteenth century in the Jones & Laughlin Steel Corporation of Pittsburgh, although James Laughlin himself had not worked for the corporation. Until 1978, when it was purchased by Ling-Temco, it was one of the four largest steel companies in the United States.

❦

70. TLS-1

Nov. 19/60

Dear Denise

Do say to Elizabeth McFarland that I suggested your name with the highest recommendations I am capable of. I wish only that you could make the trip to Philadelphia to present the poem or poems in person. I have never met the lady but she seems a person you would profit by meeting.

Her name and address is:

Elizabeth McFarland, The Ladies' Home Journal, Independence Square, Philadelphia 5, Penna.

By the way your notice of "A" in POETRY was magnificent!

Yours
Bill

Elizabeth McFarland   McFarland (married to the poet Daniel Hoffman) left the position of poetry editor in August 1961, "fired, actually, in a palace revolution…[when] a young man from Iowa replaced Editor in Chief Bruce Gould, whose aim had been to bring good poets to the American housewife. Would that D.L. had been one of them" (letter to Christopher MacGowan, November 17, 1997).

notice of "A"   DL reviewed Louis Zukofsky's *"A" 1–12* (Kyoto, Japan: Origin Press, 1959) in her essay "A Necessary Poetry," *Poetry* 97, 2 (November 1960), pp. 102–9, generally praising the poem, although with some qualifications about its overall structure and occasional obscurity. The book includes a short, 1957, essay by WCW on Zukofsky that DL quotes with approval in her notice. LZ himself was unhappy with DL's review, "because <u>he</u> thought I should have asked him about anything I didn't understand, which to <u>my</u> mind would have been quite dishonorable. I shall always think I was quite right!" (Notes 1997).

❧

71. *ALS-6*

277 Greenwich St. N.Y. 7
Dec. 3d. [1960]

Dear Bill & Floss,

Thanks so much for Ladies H.J. address. I just got back from a 3-day visit to Muhlenberg College—I wanted to tell you about it because Dr. Kinter who has the Poetry Workshop and Dr. Bouma who also teaches there want to come to see you one of these days. The thing is that it was a quite marvellous experience for me to be there—there's so much <u>response</u> among the kids there, even tho' they are not writing anything really good and are rather indiscriminate in their admirations—but they're <u>alive</u>, & fresh, they ask questions all the time, & the whole atmosphere was so warm & pleasant—and all this is due to these 2 men (especially Kinter) who have no professorial <u>airs</u> but sit around talking with students over coffee in the Student Center and expose their own poems for criticism in the workshop and infuse their own curiosity into the very air of the place.

I feel that their taste & knowledge concerning modern poetry is very <u>unsure</u> but what matters is that wonderful aliveness and kindly fostering interest in their students—and their lack of pretentiousness. It seems they have felt shy about coming to visit you but I told them I thought you would enjoy meeting them so this is a sort of (unsolicited) introduction and they will be writing to you.

A young chap called Charles Hanna is a recent graduate & he has I believe written to you. I had a wonderful Syrian meal cooked by his mother, and admired his little printing press in the basement on which he plans to do all sorts of wonders.

I wanted to see if I could lure you over here while the good weather holds, but my 2 Pennsylvanian reading trips caused me to let my housework fall behind terribly; also Mitch has a sore throat; so I won't attempt it until after Xmas—but hope to come to see you briefly before then—also to find out when you are going to take your New York vacation. January?

With love always,
your Denise.

Dr. Kinter and Dr. Bouma ... Charles Hanna   William Lewis Kinter (1915–1995) and J. Gysbert Bouma (who wrote his M.A. thesis on WCW's prose at the University of Pennsylvania, 1956). The following year DL published a poem in Hanna's journal *Damascus Road:* "A letter to William Kinter of Muhlenberg" (*Damascus Road* 1 [1961], pp. 15–16 (in *JL* and *Poems 1960–1967*). Kinter resigned from Muhlenberg College in June 1962, following some years of friction with the administration over a number of matters, including some of the readings that he arranged by contemporary poets. He wrote to DL of his resignation that he was "bounced for defending the Liturgy & Poetry" (August 28, 1962, at S). Charles Shahoud Hanna (b. 1934), now an attorney, had graduated from Muhlenberg in 1960. His Damascus Road Press published *Damascus Road* (1961–82) for ten issues, and included DL in one of its occasional anthologies, *10 Women: Their Poems* (1972).

72. TLS-1

Dec. 6/60

Dear Denise:

Your trip to Muhlenberg sounds good and I've already heard from them direct—something seems shaping up there, I'll hear from them again.

Whenever you have anything to say, do write. Sore throats can be hell, give Mitch my condolences.

Love
Bill

heard from them Kinter wrote to DL August 28, 1962: "Did Hanna tell you we had house visit with Dr. Williams in Rutherford? I was awe struck.... He autographed two books—one for Muhlenberg Library, one for me ..." (S).

73. ALS-3

277 Greenwich St NY 7
Jan 31st 61

Dear Bill & Floss,

Good news for Mitch at last! Horizon Press has signed a contract with him & will be publishing his novel next October—$500 advance, option on 2 books, probable paperback reprint. Viva!

I know you will rejoice with us.

How have you been faring in this cold? It just paralyzes me—and we've all had the snuffles of course. Are you going to spend a week or so in the city? I want to come to see you soon & show you various things—and Mitch will come too—getting a publisher has perked him up considerably. Enclosed is a new poem I think you may like. I reworked the one you felt was too loose, I don't know if you remember it at all, it began with my taking the clean clothes off the washline on our roof on a windy night. But I'll show you that when I see you.

Love—

Denise.

a new poem...too loose   The reworked poem is "From the Roof," see letter #68 above, while the "new poem" could be "Matins" (*JL* and *Poems 1960– 1967*), published in *Poetry* in October 1961, and with the B correspondence.

❧

74. TLS-1

Feb. 2/61

Dear Denise:

That's wonderful news as it concerns Mitch because as it concerns him it is also a triumph for you. I am very happy, we'll see its effect in the blossoming of your verse.

The coldness of the weather is a classic circumstance reminding me of Villon—and many a poet when he was young and had everything to gain or lose at the whim of the weather. When we have passed the crisis in our affairs it often happens that the impetus to be an artist is spent, I'm glad that has not been the story with Mitch. When the weather is no longer so bitter we hope you will be able to visit us.

(Interval–during which Shapiro from across the street came in to see me. An artist and brought me a small painting which I admire. I introduced him to my friend Mary Ellen Solt.)

We're going to Carnegie Hall to a violin recital by Paul Zukofsky – if I can make it.

Your reworked poem which you sent to me yesterday is very successful, I like it. Much improved after the first version.

Have to quit now before I exhaust myself against the recital this afternoon.

Love
Bill

[Note added by DL on RPL photocopy] "(acceptance of his novel.)"

Shapiro   Unidentified.

a violin recital   The recital took place on February 3, suggesting that WCW may have misdated this letter. A heavy snow storm descended on New Jersey and New York City on the afternoon of the 3rd, and WCW was unable to make the journey into the city. The seventeen-year-old Paul Zukofsky – son of poet Louis Zukofsky (1904–1978) with whom WCW had an extensive correspondence, and an occasionally close professional relationship – played to an almost empty auditorium on this his third Carnegie Hall recital. Solt was able to attend.

your reworked poem   DL's previous letter indicates that she did not enclose "From the Roof," which she had revised, and there is no typescript of the poem with the correspondence at B. WCW may be responding to the "new poem," and conflating the two.

75. *TLS-1*

277 Greenwich St. N.Y. 7
April 21 '61

Dear Bill:

Ben Raeburn, the publisher at Horizon Press, called me today and I
mentioned to him—as a kind of reassurance—that you and Floss had
read the book and liked it. He asked me if I would ask you for some
kind of statement about it, something he could use on the jacket.

I told him I was reluctant to ask. I know what you're up against and
I would—if it were altogether my own choice—not bother you with
it. But I appreciate the publisher's position. It's a small firm, with
almost no money for advertising, etc.—so this kind of thing really
matters to them. They've been very decent to me. And as far as I
know, Raeburn and J. Laughlin are about the only really honest
publishers in New York now.

Thank you again, both of you, for reading the book.

Love from us all,
Mitch

[Hand-written postscript by DL] That's a beautiful poem, the Ga-
garin one. Jay showed it to me. I loved it. Heel & toe. In fact I did
an Irish jig (heel & toe) right there in his office.

Love—
Denise

Ben Raeburn   Raeburn (c. 1911–1997) had founded Horizon Press in 1951,
and retired in 1984—the press going out of business shortly after he sold it
that year. The press, according to his obituary in *The New York Times,*
"specialized in publishing authors before they found a mass audience; au-
thors whose latest work no one else would buy and, always, books noted

for exquisite design." *The End of It* was published in England the following year by Weidenfeld and Nicolson, with U.S. paperback editions in 1963 (New American Library), 1980 (Second Chance Press, Sagaponack, NY), and 1989 (Noonday Press, N.Y.).

some kind of statement   The inside dust jacket flap of the novel carried this comment by WCW: "The reading of this novel has stirred me to the grass roots. No other account of that war has stirred me so deeply." WCW's comments were prominently displayed in advertisements for the novel. Additional endorsements included comments by Norman Mailer and Galway Kinnell.

the Gagarin one ... Jay   WCW's poem "Heel & Toe to the End," celebrating the first manned space flight on April 12th, 1961. Jay is James Laughlin. In reading this poem at the 1966 92nd St. Y tribute DL observed: "The poem with which he celebrated the first space flight, and which I had the honor to publish in *The Nation* of which I was Poetry Editor at the time, is surely a paradigm of his own experience in a life of poetry." In *Pictures from Brueghel* and *CP2*.

~~~

76. TPC

n.d. [postmark June 21, 1961]

Dear Denise:

I have gone far back since we last corresponded. It is not possible for me to describe what exactly has happened to me. It has happened very fast. Bon voyage.   Love.

Bill

gone far back   WCW had suffered another cerebral hemorrhage on June 2, and had become further limited in his ability to type or concentrate, even for limited periods. DL paraphrases WCW from this postcard in her "September, 1961" (in *O Taste and See* and *Poems 1960–1967*): 'Williams: "I can't / describe to you what has been // happening to me"'–a poem that records the passing into silence of Pound, WCW, and H.D.

❧❧

77. APC [in FW's script]

April 30/62

Dear Denise—Hurrah!—congratulations—no one ever deserved a Gug more than you!—

Love—from
Bill & Floss!

a Gug   DL was awarded a Guggenheim Fellowship for 1962–63.

❧❧

78. ALS-4

R.F.D. Temple, Maine
June 18th 62

Dear Bill and Floss

It is so lovely to have your new book, Bill, and I am thrilled and honored that you sent it to me yourself. One after another the late, the new, poems affirm themselves to your reader as living presences, each alive, even the smallest, as those little Tanagra figures of women spinning or cooking or talking together I love so much, or as some Egyptian toad or ancient Mexican carved head. The Turtle (not a 'small' poem) is one of my favorites. And Iris. One of [the] things I have always found most exciting—and I find it in these as much or even more as in the earlier poems—is that in your 'small' poems, by which I mean simply short poems that apparently focus on some single detail, there is always the reverberation of the total; not of any academic symbolism but of your vision of the world, or of what it is to be living; so that every poem is at once a complete thing, as a carved stone is, and at the same time relates to all your other poems. To my mind this is one of the marks of greatness, this

APPENDIX A

The Letters of Denise Levertov
and Florence Williams after
William Carlos Williams's Death

80. ALS-2

277 Greenwich St. N.Y. 7
March 20th 63

Dear Floss,

I would have sent this sooner but they did not send me copies until 2 days ago. It was written the day before the funeral.

Yesterday Mitch's father entered the Sons & Daughters of Israel Old Age Home on 5th Ave & 108th St. His sister is there already & it is a pleasant well-run place so we think he will be quite happy, nevertheless when the moment of parting came we felt much as we did the first time we saw Nik off to camp. Dad had been living with us for the last 6 weeks or so.

I'll call you in a week or so & see if I may visit.

Much love from Denise.

Mitch's father Irving Goodman died in January 1966.

sent this   As the following letter indicates, DL's obituary for WCW in *The Nation*, March 16, 1963, reprinted in *PW*. An offprint inscribed by DL for FW is now at RPL.

꧁꧂

81. APC

March 24 1963

Dear Denise—Of course—come out to see me. I count you our friend, just as much as if Bill were here. Thank you for your beautiful tribute in <u>The Nation</u>—it couldn't be better stated!—

My love—
Floss

꧁꧂

82. ALS-3

n.d. [March 30, 1963]

Dear Denise—

I have a small, or possibly large favor to ask of you. You sent me your beautiful tribute to Bill in the Nation.—I think I wrote and thanked you for it—However at this point I am groggy from writing to people—and I may have slipped up—

My favor is—could you send me another copy of what you wrote or ask the Nation to send one?—

Unfortunately someone—who shall be nameless—<u>must</u> have walked off with your piece <u>and</u> the copy of the Saturday Review with John Ciardi's, both of which I want for a permanent scrap book for the children. It has taught me a lesson not to let anyone handle certain papers.

Otherwise I am doing pretty well—I've been too busy to have time to think.—People in general have been wonderfully kind—and the messages of love and devotion continue to overwhelm me.—

I hope you will come out soon—tho' don't feel any pressure about it. I know you are busy.—I hope too that you & Mitch have adjusted to having his father in the "Home" for the aged.—Sometimes older people are very happy with others of their own age. My mother— while I won't say she was <u>happy</u> to be in a nursing home—certainly behaved much better than when she tried to run us—'till we just couldn't take it any more.—

My love to all of you.—

        Floss

John Ciardi's   John Ciardi (1916–1986), in his "Manner of Speaking," column, *Saturday Review of Literature,* March 23, 1963, pp. 18–20, praised WCW's "powerful part" in an age that "leaves us a golden record of American poetry."

messages   among the almost 50 that were stored in the attic of 9 Ridge Road in 1995, now at the Lilly Library, Indiana, were messages of condolence from Kenneth Burke, Hugh Kenner, Robert Lowell, Marianne Moore, Dorothy Pound, Ezra Pound, Muriel Rukeyser, Harvey Shapiro, and Louis Zukofsky.

my mother   Nannie Herman died December 20, 1949. WCW's character Gurlie Stecher in his *White Mule, In the Money,* and *The Build-Up* trilogy is loosely based upon his mother-in-law.

꧁꧂

83. ALS-4

                                Oct 8, 1963

Dear Denise—I was so happy to hear from you.—I had heard about the Vancouver conference thru Linda Wagner—who wrote me a glowing account of it and especially of your part in it. Your account is much more personal—and I can <u>see</u> each one of you—as you read —and feel your presence <u>here</u>. Bill would have been pleased. It was a beautiful tribute and all I can say is "thank you all".

I've had an up and down summer—with many petty details to settle and other annoyances—that are not settled as yet—so I have not been able to get away as I had planned.—I will go to Calif. the end of this month, alas just as you return to N.Y. I'll be gone a month or so—and will eagerly look forward to seeing you out here.—

Your name pops up here & there—I see you are going to read at the Y. this season,—and no doubt many other places.

It doesn't seem possible that Nicky is away at school. It's a very good one—and I'm sure you have no need to worry—except that all parents <u>do</u>—and especially when the chick is an <u>only</u> one. All the more reason for having him stand on his own feet among strangers.

I have a friend in Portland Maine—who sent me a copy of your beautiful tribute to Bill in 'The Nation.' His letter and yours came in the same mail. He said—"This is an excellent tribute—and if you already have it—which I assume you have—I'd like it for my scrap book." So I am returning it to him.

I hope this gorgeous weather continues for the balance of your time in Maine.—We are basking in warm sunshine and cool nights. The foliage is gorgeous—and we hopefully assume that it will continue —knowing full well that it won't!

Thank you for writing. My love to Mitch and to you—

Affectionately
Flossie

the Vancouver conference...Linda Wagner   The well-known scholar Linda Wagner-Martin, whose dissertation at Bowling Green University (1963) was on the work of WCW, and who has published studies of DL (1967), WCW's poetry (1964) and prose (1970), as well as editing *Denise Levertov: In Her Own Province* (1979) and *Interviews with William Carlos Williams* (1976). The Vancouver Poetry Conference was held at the University of British Columbia from August 5 to 12, 1963, and participants in addition to DL included Robert Creeley, Robert Duncan, Allen Ginsberg, and Charles Olson. The discussions were recorded – see *The American Poetry Archive Audio Tape Collection* catalog, San Francisco State University.

tribute   On August 12, DL, Duncan, Creeley, and Ginsberg all read poems by WCW from his later work that they particularly admired. DL read "The Ivy Crown," and "The Turtle" (in *CP2*).

read at the Y   DL read at the 92nd St. Y, New York City, on December 16, 1963.

a very good one   Putney School, Putney, Vermont, founded 1935.

❧

84. A Card S

[Christmas 1963]

HAPPY CHRISTMAS AND A PEACEFUL NEW YEAR

Dear Flossie,

We're looking forward to seeing you at that party on the 29th, we've been dying to come out & visit, hear about your California visit, etc. etc., but it has been a crazily busy fall for me; I always seem to bite off more than I can chew – underestimating the time & energy anything is going to take... There's a very nice man, Bill Rose (editor of Wyndham Lewis's Letters) who is writing a book about the avant-garde in the 20's, & would like to meet you. May I bring him out to Ridge Road some time in January? I think you'd like him, he is O.K. Would you suggest a date? Any day except Tuesdays wd be good for me & for him, but he's coming down from Boston so wd. like to know in advance. Thanks for your Xmas card, & much love from

Denise

P.S. How have you liked making that film? They have to do my bit all over again because something was wrong with the cameras. I hope it all works out well – those T.V. people are crazy.

Bill Rose   William Kent Rose (1924–1968) had edited *The Letters of Wyndham Lewis* (London, 1963; Norfolk, CT, 1964). He was teaching at Vassar at the time of his death, from an inoperable brain tumor, and the study that DL mentions remained unfinished. He was instrumental in DL being hired as a visiting faculty member for 1966–67, and his death figures in her poem "Part 1" (in *Staying Alive* and *Poems 1968–1972*).

that film   "In the American Grain," one of the *Eye on New York* series broadcast by WCBS; Executive Producer Ned Cramer, produced, written, and directed by Albert Waller, narrated by E. G. Marshall (for $11.22 and a print of the film). The program aired on the evening of February 11, 1964, and was rebroadcast the following Saturday afternoon, February 15. DL's interview – filmed in her New York apartment – is not part of the program, although FW appears in the kitchen of 9 Ridge Road, and speaks of hearing WCW sometimes tapping his feet or dancing while composing. Albert Waller reports that he interviewed Robert Lowell and Carl Sandburg for the program, in addition to DL, but at FW's suggestion – supported by Lowell – he subsequently reconceived the project and decided to let WCW's poetry speak for itself. There was nothing "wrong with the cameras" – this was a white lie, evidently Lowell's suggestion – to explain omitting the interviews to the poets. The RPL collection holds a tape of the program, which won two Emmys and the Writers Guild of America award for best script for a documentary written for American television in 1964.

❧❧❧

85. ALS-2

March 21, 1964

Dear Denise – You told me when you were here – that you are or were about to be the Poetry Editor of The Nation – again. This unity of the diverse. One can see it within single works as well as in the whole opus—the way a detail from a painting by a great painter is vital and in a sense complete, not <u>although</u> but just <u>because</u> it has an unassailable function in the larger painting. I think Frost's remark about poets being people who must 'speak of one thing in terms of another' is true but not in the way he meant it: i.e. when a poet <u>intentionally</u> does that he is <u>applying</u> symbolism—gluing it on, or scotchtaping it on. But what <u>you</u> do is to speak of things in terms of themselves, so that those <u>other things</u> come through to me (and I suppose to yourself) <u>subliminally</u> and through the interplay of one poem on another as they cast lights and shifting shadows upon one another.

I hoped and planned, as usual, to come & see you both before we left for the country, and as usual I didn't manage it because of the confusion of getting a million loose ends tied or cut off before we could leave, plus getting Nick's camp stuff ready & marked, plus tidying up for our summer tenant (young Anthony Linick, editor of <u>Nomad</u>, this year). I'm just beginning to unwind. Lilac and lily-of-the-valley were still in bloom when we got here over a week ago —they're over now but we have irises and columbines of several colors. With love

from Denise

That's a lovely photo on the cover I think.

Filed at B with carbons of "The Thread" and "Luxury," and according to a note on the file cover, two poems on two carbon leaves accompanied the letter. But these two poems had appeared in *JL,* and DL is unlikely to have sent them with this letter a year after publication. "The Thread" was composed in August 1960. See letter #65.

your new book *Pictures from Brueghel* (New York, 1962), which includes "The Turtle" and "Iris" (in *CP2*). For DL's comments on "The Turtle" see letter #28 above.

Frost's remark   DL possibly has in mind Frost's argument for metaphor as central to thought in his essay "Education by Poetry" (1930): "Poetry provides the one permissible way of saying one thing and meaning another... thinking means... saying one thing in terms of another."

Anthony Linick   *Nomad*, edited by Linick (b. 1938) and Donald Factor, ran for eleven issues, from 1959 to 1962, and published four poems by DL.

❧

79. ALS-3

277 Greenwich St N.Y. 7
March 4th, 63

Dearest Flossie

I just heard the news. I was so sad for Bill that last visit, the first of all my visits from which I did not leave exhilarated, that I can't but feel a kind of thankfulness that his so richly-lived life of creation & perception has not attenuated itself longer in that frustration of recent times. But at the same time, as you will know, I'm heavy hearted at the loss from my life of such a beloved presence.

Tonight I'm reading at U. of Rhode Island & I'll dedicate the reading to him, reading poems he liked, and some poems of his too if I feel I can read them right.

Floss, you will be in danger after such a long time of strain—like a rope giving way—look after yourself, and please accept my love and sympathy. I'll be there on Wednesday but I don't suppose I'll see you—I do hope I may come to see you soon though.

With love always,
Denise.

the news   WCW died in his sleep on March 4 of heart failure. DL wrote in
her obituary of WCW in *The Nation,* March 16: "Always I left his house in
a state of exhilaration. Except for the last time of all, a few weeks ago,
when his tongue could no longer find the words he needed for the ideas
one could see in his eyes, and he kept giving up in mid-sentence, sad and
baffled. Yet even then, vague as he had become about many things, there
remained that eagerness to hear a new poem, that acute, *distinguishing* lis-
tening. Concerning dates and events he was more confused that day than I
had ever seen him, but poetry remained in pristine focus" (*PW,* p. 255).
According to DL's datebook at Stanford her last visit to WCW was on the
afternoon of Jan 25, 1963.

on Wednesday   Funeral services for WCW were held in Rutherford on
Wednesday, March 7, before his burial at nearby Hillside Cemetery,
Lyndhurst.

morning I opened the March copy of Poetry & found the statement
—that Bill's poem "Cezanne" had been published in The Nation.

I can't tell you how ashamed I am.—all I can say is—that Bill had a
folder in his desk marked—poems unpublished. I never gave it an-
other tho't—will you <u>please</u> apologize to The Nation for me—and
tell them that I am reimbursing 'Poetry' for the awful mistake.

How are you?—Do plan to come out <u>soon</u> and bring some one with
you—if not your family!—I'm going to take a quick trip to Norway
this summer with my sister—all the way to the North Cape.—We
being Norwegian should experience it before we are too stiff in the
joints Charlotte being 3 years older than I.

> My love to all of you—
> Floss

Poetry Editor   DL was Poetry Editor of *The Nation* in 1961, and again from
1963–65.

"Cezanne"...'Poetry'   WCW's poem "Cézanne" had appeared in *The Na-
tion* in its May 13, 1961, issue. But the January 1964 issue of *Poetry* printed
it, along with "The Moral," with a note that both were unpublished (both
in *CP2*).

my sister   Charlotte Herman (c. 1889–1981)

❧❧

86. A PC

Apr 25/64

Dear Denise—I did so enjoy your visit—which was all <u>too short</u>. I
had hoped you would read some of your poems—but we just didn't
get around to it—so I took the book up to bed with me and had a re-
warding hour.—I'll write some time later.

I have mailed your pen—which was left on the table. I know you'll want it—so you should have it promptly.—

Thanks for coming—
            Love—Floss

the book   Probably an advance copy of DL's *O Taste and See* (1964). Publication date was June 4.

🙦🙤

87. APC

[Norway—stamp and postmark removed]
July 6 [1964]

It's a <u>wonderful</u> trip. We are enjoying every minute of it. At present we are half-way to the North Cape.

                    Best to all—
                    Floss

🙦🙤

88. ALS-5

As from 277 Greenwich St N.Y. 7—
actually, though, in Baltimore and on my way to Chicago!
Nov. 11th 64

Dear Flossie,

I just finished this poem, which is for you, yesterday. It was a long time a-brewing. Perhaps it is a kind of flower-sketch of Bill.

I thought of you often during the summer and was so pleased to get your p.c. from Norway. We got back to N.Y. from Maine Oct 25th and my intention was to call you during the first week & arrange a

visit & hear about your trip & everything, but between cleaning up
the apartment & various jobs (my <u>Nation</u> work etc.) I was swept
into the N.Y. maelstrom—and now I'm away for 10 days to do some
readings. I'll call you soon after I get back though. Nik & the Cree-
leys' daughter (14) who is a freshman at the Northfield School will
be coming for Thanksgiving. Nik started writing poems during the
summer—I'll show you some.

Much love—Denise.

For Floss

Brown and silver, the tufted
rushes hold sway
by the Hackensack

and small sunflowers
freckled with soot
clamber out of the fill

in gray haze of
Indian summer
among the paraphernalia

of oil refineries, the crude
industrial débris,
leftover shacks

rusting under dark
wings of Skyway—

tenacious dreamers
sifting the wind
day and night, their roots

in seeping waters;

and fierce in each disk
of coarse yellow the archaic
smile, almost
agony, almost

a boy's grin.

From Denise
Nov. 1964

P.S. I don't know if you know it, but 'archaic smile' is a specific term, i.e. the smile (which Rilke called a 'pollen-smile') on the faces of the archaic Greek Apollo's, Kore's, & maybe some other figures, which is so stylized but so full of mysterious meaning, is apparently called by archaeologists 'the archaic smile'.

D.

this poem   Published in *Fubbalo* in Summer 1965, *The Sorrow Dance* (1967), and *Poems 1960–1967* with no significant changes from this text.

Creeley's daughter   Kirsten Creeley, who graduated from Northfield Mount Hermon School, Massachusetts, in 1968.

which Rilke called   In a letter of February 20, 1914, to Lou Andreas-Salomé, "I cannot bring to mind the smile of the Egyptian gods without the word 'pollen' occurring to me." *Selected Letters of Rainer Maria Rilke: 1902–1926*, trans. R.F.C. Hull (London, 1947), p. 240.

❧

89. ALS-2

Nov 21/64

Dear Denise—

what a beautiful, moving poem!—It is a sketch of Bill!—How thoroughly he would have appreciated it and been moved by it as I am. —Thank you so much.

I expect your tour has been a triumph! I read about you more and more,—and I always say—Amen—to all the praise—so richly deserved—

Wonderful that Nick and Creeley's daughter will be with you for the holiday! I'll be waiting to hear from you at your convenience.

In the meantime my love and thanks.

Floss

❧❧

90. *A PC*

[Charlotte Amalie, St. Thomas
U.S. Virgin Islands]
n.d. [March 21st or 31st, 1966]

What a shame that you couldn't join me. It's a wonderful spot & [Trane? Tracie?] has made things easy for me to get about. Hope to see you when I return. Best to you & Mitch. Floss

❧❧

91. *A PC*

n.d. [April 1966?]

Dear Denise—Delighted to see you Wednesday afternoon. I won't ask you for lunch because I'm on a very strict diet for the present but we can have a cup of coffee or a drink. I have a copy of The <u>el corno emplumado</u> thank you just the same.—So I'll see you Wed.— as early in the afternoon as you can make it.—

Floss

el corno emplumado Published in Mexico. The April 1966 issue, #18, carried a translation of WCW's "Asphodel, that Greeny Flower" (in *CP2*) into Spanish by Rosa del Olmo and Hector Silva on pp. 189–213, and FW may be referring to this.

❦

92. ALS-2

Oct 11/66

Dear Denise—Of course I'm not alarmed at your using excerpts of Bill's letters. As far as I'm concerned use anything at any time for whatever you may want or need to use.—

Mme. Ollier will be staying with me for a week or so—I think she's coming to-morrow. I'll give her your note—in fact she may call me from N.Y. and I'll give her your phone no.—I <u>hope</u> she is as charming & considerate as her letters indicate! It's always a gamble—taking in strangers but it's no fun <u>always</u> playing safe! If you know what I mean. Had a fairly miserable summer with my gall bladder—but it's better now.

I'll be looking forward to seeing you here—but surely at the Y.M.H.A. I wouldn't miss that even if I had to be taken on a stretcher!

Love—

Floss

excerpts of Bill's letters....Y.M.H.A.   DL presented a tribute to WCW at the New York 92nd St. Y on November 20, 1966, along with Robert Lowell, at which she read excerpts from WCW's letters to her, and read and commented on a number of WCW's poems. (See introduction for more details.) Photocopies of DL's "Notes for Y Homage" (four pages), which contain most of her comments, and "Extracts from William Carlos Williams's Letters (for Y evening)" are now at RPL, having been sent to FW by DL with the July 31, 1968, letter below. The 92nd St. Y archives holds a recording of the event. A fuller selection of extracts subsequently appeared in *Stony Brook* 1–2 (1968). The evening concluded with a showing of Albert Waller's film "In the American Grain"; see letter #84.

Mme Ollier   Professor Jacqueline Ollier is currently Professor of Literature at the University of Nice, and author of *William Carlos Williams: L'homme et l'oeuvre poétique* (Nice, 1979) as well as translator of a bilingual edition of selected WCW poems.

❧❧❧

93. ALS-2

277 Greenwich St. New York, 10007
March 31st 1967

Dear Flossie,

I was waiting for some hard-cover copies of this to arrive, but as they have not, decided to send you this paperback instead rather than wait any longer.

Ever since that evening at the Y I have also been meaning to have Bill's letters to me xeroxed, & bring you a set, as you said you would like to have them; but have been so much behind with everything that I've not managed it. I feel as if I were caught in one of those dreams in which one is running after a bus which one can't catch up with & which keeps turning corners. However, in June it will stop, or rather, I will stop running after it – & we'll begin a whole year off.

I'll definitely either send or bring the xeroxed letters before then. I'm going to go & stay up at Vassar for the next few weeks as Mitch will be in California (teaching in a special project at Stanford). Nik is waiting to hear if he has been accepted at the Rhode Island School of Design.

Hope you like the new book. The poem at the very end (as you'll see) is not by me but by my sister. Love. – Denise

of this *The Sorrow Dance*, the final poem of which, "The Ballad of My Father," is by Olga Levertoff (1914–1964).

special project at Stanford MG was one of eight "writer-teachers" who took part in the federally funded "Voice Project," which explored ways to integrate speech more fully into the teaching of college composition classes (see *Voice Project: An Experiment in Teaching Writing to College Freshmen*, Stanford University, August 1967). DL is listed as one of ten "Consultants" to the project.

꧁꧂

94. ALS-4

n.d. [January 13 1968]
c/o Feibleman, 12, E. 97th St., New York 29, N.Y.
(our own apt. is sublet for the year.)

Dear Floss,

Forgive my long silence. I have been away from N.Y. since the spring. Last April when Mitch went out to California for 2 months (to teach in a special program at Stanford) I moved up to Vassar where I was teaching, (instead of commuting from New York). At the end of May I went out to join Mitch on the West coast, & we got back just in time for Nik's graduation from Putney & his 18th birthday (which coincided). Then we went straight up to Maine. We had a very busy summer. Nik went to Europe (& had a marvellous time) and I was editing the War Resisters League Peace Calendar for 1968 (I'll get you a copy)—while Mitch was beginning to prepare the anti-war action that took place at the Dept. of Justice the day before the Pentagon March. In October we were in Washington for that and for the March itself—also I was there for another thing, of quite a different kind—a conference on Poetry & Myth at the National Cathedral (a discussion in which the participants were poets & theologians).

Then we went back to Maine & stayed till the beginning of December when Mitch came down to N.Y. and I left on a tour that took me to Arizona, Kentucky, Chicago, and Minnesota. Very interesting. I got to N.Y. in time for the Xmas vacation and expected to call you & come out to see you, but we had the 'flu. And then on Jan 5th came the news of Mitch's indictment (along with Dr. Spock etc.) about which I presume you have read. And this has meant 100000 phone calls, meetings with lawyers, news conferences, T.V. crews, etc. etc. This Sunday night (tomorrow) there is a big supportive meeting at Town Hall, and then on the 15th I'm going to

Washington for the women's march on the Capitol (the so-called Jeanette Rankin Brigade) & perhaps will get arrested but if not will return to N.Y. Tues.

After that—i.e. by the end of the coming week—I should have a clearer period & would be very glad if you could—after such a long absence!—make time for me to come out & see you. I want to bring you a little Zuni fetish—a tiny animal to add to your collection—which I got for you while I was in Arizona. As you'll gather, a great deal of our time & energy these days is going into war-resistance, but of course I've been writing too & will bring a few poems along to read to you.

Nik, I forgot to say, is at the Rhode Island School of Design & is doing well so far.

I've been re-reading 'In the Money'—it is really marvellous.

Well, I hope to see you pretty soon so will not write any more now. I'll call you towards the end of the coming week.

Love from Denise.

P.S. By the way, we are not upset by the indictment because we feel it is very important for the anti-war, anti-draft movement. It brings the issue into the open & is a sort of rallying-point for activists & sympathizers. The arraignment is set for Jan. 29th—the trial may not be until the fall.

Vassar   DL describes her experience teaching at Vassar, and teaching generally, in a 1970 essay, "The Untaught Teacher," reprinted in *PW*.

War Resisters League Peace Calendar   *1968 Peace Calendar & Appointment Book: Out of the War Shadow: An Anthology of Current Poetry,* compiled and edited by DL (New York: War Resisters League, 1967). Contains by

DL "Editor's Preface" and the poem "The Altars in the Street" (in *Poems 1960–1967*).

action...March   On Friday October 20, 1967, MG was part of a group leading a protest against the draft at the Department of Justice by soliciting draft cards and turning them in to the Department. On the following day a crowd variously estimated at 35,000–60,000 marched on the Pentagon to protest the war in Vietnam. For their part in the Department of Justice protest, and other anti-draft activities, MG, along with William Sloane Coffin, Michael Ferber, Marcus Raskin, and Dr. Benjamin Spock were indicted on January 5, 1968, by a Grand Jury in Boston for advocating resistance to the draft law—a charge that carried the possibility of up to five years imprisonment and a $10,000 fine. These are among a number of the events DL alludes to in this and following letters that appear in her *To Stay Alive* (1971).

a conference   DL's talk for this conference "convened to discuss parable, myth, and language under the sponsorship of the Church Society for College Work" was later published in *The Anglican Review*, L.3 (1968) and is reprinted in *PW* as "The Sense of Pilgrimage." In the essay DL notes that the influence of WCW's work upon her own did not include "the profound mythic element" in his verse. The proceedings, with some records of the discussions that followed the papers, were published as *A Meeting of Poets & Theologians to Discuss Parable, Myth & Language* (Washington D.C.: The Advance Program, Washington Cathedral & The Church Society for College Work, c. 1967).

meeting at Town Hall   the January 14 rally at Town Hall, W. 43rd St., New York City, attracted 1500 supporters, according to *The New York Times* report the following day.

women's march...arrested   On January 15, 5,000 women led by 87-year-old former member of Congress Jeanette Rankin (the first woman elected to Congress) protested the war in Vietnam on Capitol Hill on the opening day of Congress. There were no arrests reported.

In the Money   The second novel in WCW's *White Mule* trilogy, originally published in 1940, had been reissued in 1967.

❦

95. *ALS-2*

Jan 21/68

Dear Denise—I was very happy to hear from you.—I had been wondering about you.—I had read something of your activities but rather sketchily, so was not convinced that all was well. You surely have been active, and my admiration goes out to you & Mitch for what you are doing. I have just day before yesterday returned from the Hospital.—I took a tumble for myself two weeks ago—dislocated & chipped my left shoulder—& got a very bad bruise to the left side of my face.—It's a nuisance but—I have good help at home now—& I trust it won't take more than the usual 6 weeks to give me back the use of my arm.—Anytime you can spare a few hours & the <u>weather</u> is <u>decent</u> I'd love to see you & hear you read & talk. Bless you.—

My love to both of you.

As ever.
Floss

❦

96. *TLS-6*

July 31 68
Temple, Maine 04984

Dear Floss,

Ages ago—at the time of the Memorial Program at the Y 2 years ago, that is—I asked you if you would like copies of Bill's letters to me, from which I made extracts for that occasion; and I must apologize for never sending them: I got xeroxes made and somehow put them in a drawer and thought I'd sent them but long since realised I had not, yet still procrastinated. I have never shown them to anyone but a few close friends, and keep the originals in a bank box. Bill said far too many dear and complimentary things about my work for me to think of publishing them or letting a library have them, at least until I am very old, since it would seem like selfadvertisement.

However, as well as finally sending them to you, I do want to ask if it would be alright with you if I let a few of the <u>extracts</u> (the 'impersonal' things about writing—as arranged (more or less) for that Y evening, be published in the first issue of Stony Brook, which is being edited by a young poet who is a close friend. As well as the extracts he would like to use the letter of Feb. 16. 58 which, though it quotes from a poem of mine, I have been persuaded would <u>not</u> look like a self-advertisement. I am underlining the date in red so that you will be sure to know which one I mean. <u>I most certainly won't let him use <u>any</u> unless you give your approval</u>. I'll be grateful if you can let me know soon.

We are happily rusticating after the extraordinary experience of the trial, which was like living in public for a month and more—. The outcome was not a shock at all and I hope you were not too concerned. I should have written sooner—but was paralyzed as far as writing <u>anything</u> while the whole process was going on, and have plunged into poetry (thank god) since it ended, and am only just emerging into ordinary life, I mean into being able to do more than one thing at a time...

Mitch and the others are now out on appeal, and the circuit court of appeals won't even begin hearing the case till the new year, so we have quite a long stretch of relative calm before us. I'm going to Mexico on the 12th for my long delayed visit to my mother—will be back at the end of the month. (If you don't write about the reproduction of those letter-extracts before the 12th, would you mind addressing your reply to me there, so I can let George Quasha know?—the address wd. be, c/o Mrs Levertoff, Crespo 313, Oaxaca, Oax., Mexico. Postage is the same as for U.S. and Canada.)

I saw Sister Bernetta Quinn in Seattle in April and have had a couple of good letters from her too. I gather all is excitement with Jim and Ann as Leila's wedding approaches – this Saturday, isn't it? We saw Leila and her Daniel a couple of times while we were living in Cambridge for the trial, and he is really nice. J. seems very pleased to get such a congenial son-in-law.

Nik is Europe tenting with his girl-friend. When last heard of they were washing their hair and dishes in the Rhône just across from the Pont d'Avignon.

Mitch has not been able to return to work on his novel yet after the political activity of the last 8 months, but has been writing some poems, and I think they are awfully good. I wish Bill could have seen them, I think he would have liked them. I will send you some.

He is also working on an anthology of documents on civil disobedience and non-violence etc., for which he has written a brilliant first draft of an introduction. He's waiting to hear if MacMillan is going to give him a contract for it. It interests him very much, and also will be a possible source of income if it is done right – which we'll need, as though the ACLU and the defense fund are taking care of legal expenses we have had a lot of incidental costs, also Our Boy didn't keep up his grades too well at the Rhode Island School of Design and it seems that though he is reaccepted for the coming year he has lost his scholarship ... This was at least partly due to his having a girlfriend in New York. You know what they're like at that age. If only she were in Providence too they might have done some studying together – but as it was he spent his weekends running down to see her. I guess you're only young once, but we feel a little irritated with him at the moment. When he's actually present, with his big eyes, it's hard to be mad at him – though god knows I used to be when he was little ...

How are you? You still had your arm in a sling when I last saw you. Has it been stiff since, or did it go back to normal? I do hope so.

We feel sad because we finally worked out a plan to straighten out my mother's visa etc and have her come here to Maine, for a couple of months, but her doctor will not let her make the trip. She is not ill, but he feels at her age and with some high bloodpressure the change of climate and elevation would be too great a risk to take. In the past it would have been too primitive here (outhouse etc.) for her comfort, but we now have a little bathroom (not quite finished yet) and a screened porch, so once here I believe she would have enjoyed it. But it can't be done. We are more disappointed than she is, though, fortunately.

Hope to hear from you soon—and as to those letters, whatever you say goes.

> Much love,
> Denise

in a bank box…sending them   The letters from WCW entered the Stanford University collection, probably with the initial purchase from DL in 1988, while the photocopies sent to FW are now in the RPL collection.

Stony Brook…a young poet   *Stony Brook* was edited by poet and editor George Quasha (b. 1942). The journal reproduced the letter of February 16, 1958.

the outcome   At the trial, which began on May 20 and lasted until June 14, in Federal District Court in Boston, Raskin was acquitted, while the other four were found guilty and sentenced on July 10 to two years imprisonment, with $5,000 fines for Coffin, MG, and Spock. On July 11, 1969, the United States Court of Appeals for the First Circuit, in Boston, subsequently overturned the convictions. The charges against Spock and Ferber were dismissed, but not those against Coffin and MG—nevertheless the prosecution was not renewed.

Sister Bernetta Quinn Sister Bernetta Quinn, OSF (b. 1915) teacher, poet and scholar of the Catholic Church, and of modernist poetry, whose *The Metamorphic Tradition in Modern Poetry* (New Brunswick, N.J., 1955) includes one of her essays on WCW's work.

Jim, Ann, Leila, Daniel James Laughlin and his second wife, Ann Resor. Leila Laughlin married Daniel Javitch on August 3, 1968.

Mitch...some poems...an anthology of documents MG's book of poems *Light From Under a Bushel* (New York, 1968) was privately printed. The anthology, *The Movement Toward a New America,* appeared two years later (New York and Philadelphia, 1970), with an introduction, "What's Happening," by MG that identifies WCW as one of the "crucial sources" for "the first wave of a new vitality in the sub-culture [that] came with the new poetry of the 50's and 60's" – particularly his *In the American Grain* and *Paterson.* Macmillan did not publish the anthology.

❧❧

97. ALS-4

313 Crespo, Oaxaca, Oax., Mexico
n.d. [August 1968]

Dear Flossie,

Thanks so much for your lovely & generous letter and for the check. It came before I left Maine for Mexico but I had a family of 4 (2 little boys) visiting during the last 3 days I was home & between seeing to them & trying to pack & shop for the things I wanted to take as gifts, I didn't manage to thank you. Kids <u>will</u> leave screen doors open & let flies & mosquitos in & I was driven quite distracted running around shutting them behind them!

I accept the $50 with many thanks on behalf of the Defense Fund which is not only paying <u>our</u> legal expenses but trying to help many obscure young men as well.

My mother is little changed, really, in the 3 years since I've seen her, although she's been quite ill in the intervening time with high blood-pressure & a slight case of diabetes. Both seem to be under control, she takes some pills for each daily & is mentally as vigorous as ever. This morning when I came into her room she had Macaulay's Essays propped up against her teapot to read with her breakfast.

George Quasha will be overjoyed at being able to print those excerpts from Bill's letters—I wrote to tell him he may.

I hope the post-concussion depression has disappeared by now. When I saw you last I didn't realize the extent to which you'd been concussed—you didn't seem depressed then—but I expect it is a sort of delayed action effect.

The youngest child of the Mexican family my mother has lived with these past 11 years is 11 now and speaks English charmingly. My mother has brought her up on the English children's classics—and American too, such as <u>Little Women</u>—and when she's 15 or so I hope to have her come to us for a year & go to school in the U.S., if things work out & the world is not by then in a state of total upheaval or worse. It's funny how sometimes one feels so despairing & yet almost at the same time continues to make such plans...I guess one has to have that much optimism to live at all.

I'll be back the end of the month, & Nik will be back from his adventures in Europe—had a lovely letter from him today.

Love—Denise

98. *ALS*-2

July 30/69

Dear Denise—Due to the miserable weather our trip has been delayed. If all goes well—we will stop to see you & Mitch—on the 14th —to spend the night if we may. We go up the coast of Maine to Nova Scotia & will see you on the way back.

I'll call you before I leave here—so that there will be no mix up.

Let's hope for good weather we are just a lot of drowned-rats! I've never seen so much rain & such <u>heavy</u> showers. No water shortage this summer! It will be good to see you. Emily & I are looking forward to our visit.

Love to both of you
Floss

Emily Emily Mitchell Wallace, who had met FW and WCW while preparing her *A Bibliography of William Carlos Williams* (Middletown, CT, 1968).

⚘

99. *ALS-2*

Aug 18/69

Dear Denise & Mitch—

I'm not exaggerating when I say—staying with you was the highlight of our tour! I'm sure Emily agrees. She was talking in superlatives about you and I agreed with every word! The mushrooms— the raspberries so delicious & not to be bought at any price!

I'm sorry my stability is what it is—and I am grateful for your kindness in letting me have your room. I'm much better now that I am not driving all day. Please remember I have a guest room and I couldn't have more welcome guests than you. Stay as long as you like. I mean it.

Mitch I'll be thinking about you rooting for you & talking to all the youngsters I can lay my hands on.

>My love to both of you—
>Floss

※※

100. A Card S

Dec 29/69

Dear Denise—your belated Xmas card came to-day—<u>with</u> your address which I did not have before!—I had wondered why I hadn't heard from you earlier. Anyway—Jan 25—1970 will be a <u>RED LETTER</u> day. I'll be looking forward to it—you & your friends. Of course stay over nite or as many more as you wish. It will be a delight to have you here.—How about Mitch?

Happy New Year
>Affectionately
>Floss

※※

101. A L S-1

June 9/71

Dear Denise—

Much happiness in the new <u>move</u>. You get farther & farther away from me—but I can take it! Thank you for the article about the jail experience. Do be careful <u>about you</u>. I'm all for what you are doing

—wish I could join you but I can scarcely write. My fingers are so stiff! <u>Damn.</u> Best to you & Mitch—

Love
Floss

the new move   DL had been artist-in-residence at Kirkland College, Clinton, N.Y. for the 1970–71 academic year.

article about the jail experience   Unidentified.

❧

102. A Card S

n.d. [1971?]

Dear Denise—Thank you for remembering me with your delightful book "To Stay Alive." I have just read here & there so far and find some very beautiful. I do like The Olga Poems—they are very moving—

Enjoy the holidays if possible? I think of you & Mitch & Nick very much—may your ties remain close.

Affectionately—
Floss

"To Stay Alive"   *To Stay Alive* (1971) begins with a suite of poems titled "Olga Poems," written at the time of Olga Levertoff's death in 1964 (in *Poems 1968–1972*).

ties remain close   After some difficult years in their relationship, MG and DL separated in 1973, divorcing in 1975, and in 1980 he married Sandra Gregor, with whom he had a son, Matthew. Mitchell Goodman died of pancreatic cancer February 1, 1997, in Temple, Maine.

❧

103. *TLS-4*

[4 Glover Circle
W. Somerville, MA]
n.d. [May 1974]

[first 2 pages missing]

platform dripping wet from the snow). And the friend I stayed with had just gone through a painful divorce, so when I did get myself together next day it seemed essential to stick around and talk and listen to her....And so it goes: I didn't call you because I saw no realistic prospect of getting to see you, and I have difficulty just <u>chatting</u> on the telephone; I get all tongue-tied.

The teaching job I have this year (and will have next year too) at Tufts is pleasant but quite a bit more time consuming than some I have had. My bigger course has 70 students in it, and even with an assistant that means a large number of papers to read (we split them evenly, and switch each time so that I get to read some of each student's work). During the year I have visited my mother a couple of times—she is celebrating her 89th birthday on June 29th so I will be going again for that. She has trouble with her feet, and her eyesight is poor—though she still is able to read and paint, thank god. But it hurts me to see how slowly she has to read, poring over the words which she can only make out with difficulty. Mitch is still working on that novel and is spending a lot of time in Maine. Nik, who will be 25 next month, has been staying here while working on a lithography job (printing some Baskin limited editions, portraits of American Indians) and is an absolute joy to have around. He has grown into a really wonderful person and I feel as if I am experiencing now a lot of the joy in my son that—due to anxiety, irritability, and so forth—I failed to experience fully when he was a child. I think I wrote to you about his visiting his grandmother last year— she too found him to have grown into a delightful young man and she wrote to me that he was '<u>a wise person</u>', which I thought was an unusual and beautiful realization for an 88 year old grandmother to have about a grandchild.

I'm not at all certain that you ever received a copy of The Poet in the World, a book of prose pieces of mine which J. published a few months ago. My intention was to mail you the first advance copy (because there is a previously unpublished little essay on Bill in it, as well as the one I wrote as an obituary which appeared in The Nation). I remember being undecided as to whether to mail it or hold it until I saw you (which at that point I was expecting to do—this was January—) and I cant remember whether when my January visit did not materialize I ever did mail it. Oh dear. If so, please forgive me and please accept the copy I am now mailing (in separate envelope). I feel especially badly about it because the whole time that book was in preparation I imagined myself presenting it to you and wondered if you would like/approve the Williams essay, and hoped you would. There is a lot more I would like to write about him—this is only a small beginning. I read a lot of the poems—focussing on earlier poems which have been neglected—in my lectures last fall and it was so exciting and nourishing.

I guess this is enough of this long ramble. Please don't tire yourself by answering unless you happen to feel like writing, will you? But if you could get someone to drop me a line to say how you are I would be much obliged. Much much love dear Flossie. From

Denise.

I now have hopes of getting down to visit you one day between my visit to my mother & my trip to England (for rest & the renewal of some of my old friendships) but will wait till I know just when I can do it before checking out with you whether you would find it convenient. I do long to see you, it has been such ages...

teaching job   initially a Visiting Professor, DL received tenure at Tufts University, Massachusetts, teaching there from 1972 to 1978.

my mother following the death of Beatrice Spooner-Jones Levertoff on June 8, 1977, DL founded in Oaxaca, and sought funding for, the Fundación Beatrice A. Levertoff Centro de Rehabilitación Visual.

Baskin limited editions Printmaker and sculptor Leonard Baskin (b. 1922), who had a summer home in Maine, executed a series of American Indian portraits between 1972 and 1975.

The Poet in the World ... J. New Directions published the volume of essays in 1973. The previously unpublished essay on WCW, "Williams and the Duende," (pp. 257–66) had been given as a lecture at the University of Cincinnati in the spring of 1973. DL records that although when she first read WCW's work it deepened "some latent capacity in myself to see the world more freshly: yet my strongest sense of his vision, as I grow older, is of the way it encompasses the dark, the painful, the fierce." The essay also makes a claim for the importance of WCW's earlier work, and regrets the tendency in colleges to present WCW only through the tiresomely familiar and basically unrevealing anthology "specimens," such as "The Red Wheelbarrow" and "The Yachts."

❦

104. Mailgram

5/21/76
New York NY 100

DENISE LEVERTOV
4 GLOVER CIRCLE
SOMERVILLE MA 02144

TRIED TO REACH YOU BY PHONE. I KNOW YOU WOULD WANT TO KNOW. FLOSS WILLIAMS DIED PEACEFULLY WEDNESDAY MORNING MAY 19

FRED
NEWBOOKS
11:28 EST

Fred Frederick Martin, a Vice President of New Directions, worked for the publisher from 1967 to 1983.

APPENDIX B

Three Letters by William Carlos Williams
in Support of Denise Levertov
to the John Simon Guggenheim Memorial Foundation
1955–1960

WCW wrote letters of support for DL's unsuccessful applications to the Foundation for the 1956, 1959, and 1960 competitions.

Following a further unsuccessful application in 1961, DL was awarded a Fellowship in 1962 (see letters #15 and #77, and the fuller discussion in the introduction). Typographical errors have been silently corrected for the text below.

❧❧

November 30, 1955

Denise Levertov Goodman is a poet, a young woman, as yet an unknown quantity in the world of letters. She is of Welsh & Jewish ancestry and was born in England where she lived until recent years. She is not a scholar.

As yet she has published no book. I became acquainted with her poems in American little magazines and was immediately struck by their freedom of composition and knack of getting the domestic scene down on the page. Their humanity and dignity together with their portrayal of the life immediately about her in the terms of her art immediately won me as a listener or reader.

She feels the need to communicate her experiences as a recent comer to America and what it has meant to a woman of her parentage to her. Her moving statement of her reasons for seeking a Guggenheim Fellowship contained in this letter is her best advocate that I can think of. Since there is no adequate example of her work available to quote or tell you of I cannot go on with this report at greater length.

Denise Levertov Goodman is a young aspiring poet who has done some good work and deserves to be encouraged. That is all I can say.

❧

November 28, 1958

This is an unusually talented young woman of mixed blood, Jewish and Welsh, who spent the recent years of her life in Cornwall. She was early smitten with the poetic urge and published conventional verse in England. Living as she was able she became at first a trained nurse and devoted all her time to nursing the war wounded. But her poetic urge gave her no peace so that when she had been convinced that the "new poetry" was what she wanted she came to America, to New York, where she at once made her presence felt by publishing her verse in the little magazines that began to open their pages to her. Her knowledge about the art of verse and her willingness to embrace the freer rhythms coupled with her courage and flawless sense of time made her a winner whenever she came to grips with any who challenged her. But it is a tough job no matter how talented you are to make a hit with poetry in the modern world. Denise and her husband have had some tough sleighing in the last 4 or 5 years.

Her poems, wherever they have appeared, direct, without inversions of the phrase have been accepted as valid whenever the American idiom has been involved. They are original and unconventional in their thought and express a view of life that is sound in the terms we have to face today. She is not what may be spoken of as a "radical" save in her poetic technical, handling of the material of poetry itself. Any competent student of the English language will find material to praise. That's not saying enough, speaking of "competent student of the English language" it sounds entirely too academic for a description of Denise Levertov Goodman. She is in my opinion the best woman who is writing poetry in America today.

She has published several small books, a list of which is subjoined to this report, 3 in all, that have been widely read and praised in the U.S. so that editors know they have an artistic intelligence to deal with in this poet, equal to the best. I have read her consistently and always with the greatest pleasure—from the two or 3 years she spent in Mexico to the present. She is just beginning to discover herself and having a mind and a conscience she'll go on developing for many years to come. This sounds like a rave review but you can't spoil this woman that way. She has known hard living, she has known the New York back streets but it didn't spoil her when she had the chance in writing of The Pepper Tree which she saw, one of her loveliest poems, which she saw when she lived across the border.

No one can expect a poet to ring the bell every time she sits down with blank paper before her to realize what she has to accomplish in her poem. There are sterile periods, we can't get beyond that. Sometimes this poet comes out second best. On the other hand there are bursts of energy and perception, which show this poet to be unrivalled about us. No one can predict anything from a poet but unless I miss my guess Denise Levertov Goodman has not touched bottom yet and it will be long before she does so.

᳗᳗

January 1, 1960

With her last book, With eyes at the back of our Heads, just being published by New Directions Denise Levertoff has emerged at the age of 35 as a poet likely to produce work which will mark her as one of the most distinguished artists of her time. These most recent poems are distinguished in a way that makes them outstanding but hard adequately to praise. They are English composition with all the virtues of the classroom but raised to a height, the choice of words which distinguishes excellent work but with something added which makes them outstanding. The sheer ability of invention in the lines gives me the conviction that here at last is a poet, a woman who can be counted on to go anywhere. She'll do it too whatever may be made against her, don't worry—though at the moment she can use the assistance you may accord her.

I haven't had in years the conviction of energy and chained power that this woman gives me—perfectly disciplined that this woman gives me. You can't stop her but you can assist her in achieving her career with honor to yourselves if you so choose.

With the reading of the opening poems of this last book something went through me that I had to acknowledge that here I was dealing with a distinguished talent—an inspired woman of rare ability. I can't go on repeating over and over again a list of the qualities that distinguish her:

Her inheritance of innate traits is unusual when you dwell on what she is and what she has made of herself, gradually, fighting herself, what had she otherwise to fight, you realize the road she has travelled. Her father was a Jew but a Jew converted to Christianity an English citizen living in Wales converted to the Church of England therefore of strong religious beliefs. Her mother was a Welsh woman. Then the man died, daughter and mother moved to this country guided by a conviction on the daughter's part that the American idiom was the language in which she wanted to school herself. Denise found herself captured by the local language to which she gave herself up and began to write poetry living in New York, gradually rounding out her craft which she has been going on doing for the last 10 or 15 years. Following her husband who for business reasons removed to Mexico she lived there with her 8 year old son for several years getting to know the Mexican peasants and developing her craft as a poet.

She has always had clearly in mind what she had to do; become a poet. Some of her poems under the Mexican environment were outstanding and got her an environment. She was getting into her thirties when the family returned to New York where they have been living for the past 4 or five years. Denise has been slow to develop her talent, plugging away at her vocabulary through the years making herself ready to be the accomplished master of her language that she is now—in which her English birth and early training have been of vast assistance to her.

But she has been a resident of the new world, a practicer of its language with increasing intensity as she developed more and more in its practices. Just at this moment she has begun to emerge as a master, ready, secure in her seat, to go to whatever may await her. Life for an artist is a continuous road of development unless he or she is arrested at some moment of his career by circumstances over which he may have no control such as initial lack of intelligence or inability to vary with the field. Levertov does not need to fear that. Being a woman, happily married with a child of her own, has its hazards for a serious artist.

It will be fascinating to follow Levertov's further development. I love and respect her genius. May she go on to make the way more exciting for most of us.

APPENDIX C

Poems Collected with the Letters

The following lists record the poems by DL that are collected with her letters to WCW at the Beinecke Library, Yale University, and the far fewer poems by WCW that are with DL's papers at Stanford. Titles are listed in order of first appearance in print unless otherwise noted, followed by the month and/or year of publication, and the first collected volume in which the poem appeared. Some of DL's poems did not receive a first periodical publication, and the DL material also includes two early drafts of published poems, and one unpublished poem. As noted in the Introduction to this edition, at both libraries the poems are filed separately from the letters (exceptions are DL's "For Floss" with letter #88, and WCW's "View of a Woman at Her Bath," with letter #37, where each formed an integral part physically of their respective letters). Since DL visited WCW on many occasions, not all poems necessarily accompanied correspondence. But where the annotations to this edition note that a poem is or may be associated with a particular letter, the letter number follows the publication data.

❧

Poems by Levertov filed with her correspondence to Williams

In Obedience (Autumn 1954, *OI*), #8
Something (Fall 1954, *OI*), #8
Merritt Parkway (Winter 1954, *OI*), #13
Mrs. Cobweb (Summer 1955, *HN*), #13

An Innocent [II, 1st. version] (Fall/Winter 1955, *CEP*), #16

A Song (1956, *OI*), #20

Laying the Dust (1956, *HN*), #22

The Springtime (1956, *OI*), #22

A Clean Bare Room (unpublished, sent March 1956), #20

The Lovers (unpublished version, sent March 1956), #20

The Lovers *HN*, #22

Courage *HN*, #27

A Silence *HN*, #27

The Marriage *HN*, #20

The Whirlwind (July/September 1957, *OI*)

The Absence (July/September 1957, *OI*)

Action (Autumn 1957, *OI*), #37

The Recognition (Winter 1957, *OI*), #20

Tomatlan (Variations), iv (Winter 1957, *HN*), #22

Le Bateleur (Winter 1957, *HN*), #22

Illustrious Ancestors (1958, *OI*), #37

A Supermarket in Guadalajara, Mexico (January 1958, *OI*), #27

The Dead Butterfly (Summer/Autumn 1958, *WE*)

Pleasures (August 1958, *WE*)

The Departure (October 1958, *WE*), #37

A Stir in the Air *OI*

Sunday Afternoon *OI*

The Sharks *OI*, #37

Broken Glass *OI*, #37

Pure Products *OI*, #37

At the Edge (January 1959, *WE*), #46

The Communion (July 1959, *WE*), #46

The 5 Day Rain (Summer 1959, *WE*)

Come into Animal Presence (April 1960, *JL*), #53

The Makers (unpublished version of "Six Variations, i," April 1960, *JL*), #52

The Dog of Art (Fall 1960, *WE*), #46

An Ignorant Person (Fall 1960, *WE*), #46

The Lagoon (*WE*), #37
Luxury (1961, *JL*)
Canticle (1961, *JL*), #62
Corazon (1961, *JL*), #62
The Weave (1961, *JL*), #62
Sierra (1961, *JL*), #62
The Jacob's Ladder (1961, *JL*), #62
The Thread (September 1961, *JL*), #66
Matins (October 1961, *JL*), #73
For Floss (Summer 1965, *The Sorrow Dance* [1967]), #88

Poems by Williams filed with Levertov's papers

View of a Woman at Her Bath (Fall 1957, in *Pictures from Brueghel*
   [1962], as "Portrait of a Woman at Her Bath"), #37

Widower's Monologue (Winter 1959), *CP2*
The Wanderings of the Tribe (Winter 1959), *CP2*
[Both translations from the Spanish of Mexican poet Alí
   Chumacero]

Three Nahuatl Poems (1959), *CP2*
[Translated from the Spanish versions of Angel Maria Garibay]

Typescript of Paterson V (1958), dated December 4, 1957

INDEX

ACKNOWLEDGMENTS

New Directions gratefully acknowledges permission to publish quotations from the following libraries, institutions, foundations, estates, and individuals: The Lilly Library of Indiana University; The Rutherford Public Library; Stanford University Libraries (for quotations from The Denise Levertov papers, M601, as well as material still privately held, in 1998, but expected shortly to be incorporated with the Levertov papers at Stanford); The Yale Collection of American Literature, Beinecke Rare Book and Manuscript Library, Yale University; Washington University Libraries in St. Louis (for an extract from a letter sent by Denise Levertov to Mona Van Duyn in the Mona Van Duyn Papers, Special Collections, Washington University Libraries); The Poetry Center (now The Unterberg Poetry Center) of the 92nd Street Young Men's and Young Women's Hebrew Association (for taped remarks made by Denise Levertov at the 92nd St. Y on December 13, 1963); The John Simon Guggenheim Memorial Foundation; The Estate of Marianne Moore (by Marianne Craig Moore, Literary Executor); The Kenneth Burke Literary Trust (by Michael Burke, Co-Executor); The Estate of James Laughlin; Cid Corman; Robert Creeley; Elizabeth McFarland Hoffman.